Great Day Hikes
on North Carolina's
Mountains-to-Sea
Trail

Great Day Hikes

on North Carolina's

Mountains-to-Sea

Trail

THE OFFICIAL GUIDE

FROM FRIENDS OF THE

MOUNTAINS-TO-SEA TRAIL

EDITED BY JIM GRODE

THE UNIVERSITY OF NORTH CAROLINA PRESS

CHAPEL HILL

A SOUTHERN GATEWAYS GUIDE
Manufactured in the United States of America

Designed by Richard Hendel
Set in TheSans by Tseng Information Systems, Inc.

The University of North Carolina Press has been a
member of the Green Press Initiative since 2003.

Cover photographs: Open Ponds Trail, Buxton Woods,
by Beerdra; three hikers by Jerry Barker.

Library of Congress Cataloging-in-Publication Data
Names: Friends of the Mountains to Sea Trail, issuing body. | Grode, Jim, editor.
Title: Great day hikes on North Carolina's Mountains-to-Sea Trail : the official
guide from Friends of the Mountains-to-Sea Trail / edited by Jim Grode.
Other titles: Southern gateways guide.
Description: Chapel Hill : The University of North Carolina Press, 2020. |
Series: A Southern gateways guide | Includes index.
Identifiers: LCCN 2019037840 | ISBN 9781469654850 (paperback) |
ISBN 9781469654867 (ebook)
Subjects: LCSH: Hiking—North Carolina—Mountains-to-Sea Trail—Guidebooks. |
Trails—North Carolina—Mountains-to-Sea Trail—Guidebooks. | Mountains-to-Sea
Trail (N.C.)—Guidebooks. | North Carolina—Guidebooks.
Classification: LCC GV199.42.N662 F75 2020 | DDC 796.5109756—dc23
LC record available at https://lccn.loc.gov/2019037840

Southern Gateways Guide™ is a registered trademark
of the University of North Carolina Press.

CONTENTS

Great Day Hikes
on North Carolina's
**Mountains-to-Sea
Trail**

INTRODUCTION

The Mountains-to-Sea Trail (MST) offers an extraordinary way to explore North Carolina, one step at a time. Friends of the Mountains-to-Sea Trail (Friends) has produced this book to showcase single-day trips that highlight the features and diversity of the MST. We hope you will use this guide and our other resources to plan your hikes on the MST, and perhaps even be inspired to take the plunge for a longer trip, whether a short backpacking trip or a challenging trek of the entire trail.

About the Mountains-to-Sea Trail

THE TRAIL

The Mountains-to-Sea Trail is exactly what its name implies—a 1,175-mile trail that crosses North Carolina from Clingmans Dome in Great Smoky Mountains National Park near the Tennessee line to Jockey's Ridge on the Outer Banks. Ultimately, the trail will be a continuous footpath designated by the North Carolina Division of Parks and Recreation (State Parks) as a unit of the State Parks system. About 700 miles of the route—roughly 60 percent—are currently on natural surface or greenway trail, unpaved forest roads, or beach, much of it officially designated as MST by State Parks. A series of connectors on back roads knits together finished sections to span the state. A paddle route on the Neuse River provides an alternate way to complete part of the coastal plain section, from Smithfield to New Bern.

Along its way, the MST passes through thirty-seven counties, four national parks, three national forests, two national wildlife refuges, ten state parks, four state game lands, one state forest, one state historic site, and numerous local parks and protected areas, and alongside several lakes and reservoirs. Unlike many other long-distance trails, such as the Appalachian Trail or Pacific Crest Trail, the MST does not try to be a wilderness trail. Instead, it aims to trace the diversity that is North Carolina: from ancient mountains to small Piedmont farms, coastal swamps to colonial towns, barrier islands to changing textile villages, it is as much about the people and culture of the state as about the natural landscape.

HISTORY OF THE MST

In 1973, the North Carolina Trails System Act expressed the need for abundant trails "to provide for the ever-increasing outdoor recreation needs of
an expanded population and . . . promote public access to, travel within,
and enjoyment and appreciation of the outdoor, natural and remote areas
of the State." One of the act's provisions created the North Carolina Trails
Committee (NCTC) to work with State Parks "on all matters directly or in-
directly pertaining to trails, their use, extent, location, and the other ob-
jectives and purposes" of the Trails System Act.

As a result of the consultation between State Parks and NCTC, Howard N.
Lee, then the secretary of the Department of Natural Resources and Community Development, gave a speech on September 9, 1977, in which he
proposed "establishing a state trail between the mountains and the seashore in North Carolina." He envisioned that the trail would cross land
owned by the national park system, national forest system, state parks,
city and county governments, and willing private landowners interested
in providing "a legacy to future generations." The idea was to give hikers
"a real feel for the sights, sounds, and people of the state," not simply to
create a trail through the woods. The concept anticipated that costs would
be shared among local, state, and federal agencies; private owners would
donate land rights; and a strong volunteer organization would help promote, construct, and maintain the trail.

State Parks took a strong interest in the MST from its beginnings, but
the trail was not officially incorporated into the North Carolina State Park
System by a vote of the legislature until 2000. Since that time, State Parks
has helped develop regional plans for the trail route and supported construction and maintenance of the trail through grants and bond funding.
When a trail section along the planned route is opened to the public, State
Parks officially dedicates it as part of the MST.

Volunteer efforts in support of the MST were first led by the North
Carolina Trails Association (NCTA), which was informally created in 1977
and chartered in 1982 to "promote the establishment and conservation
of a system of scenic, recreational, and historic trails . . . to work with
federal, state, and local agencies and trail related organizations, landowners, and individuals in planning, acquisition, development, maintenance and proper use of trails and trail related facilities." This organization worked actively with the NCTC until the late 1980s. One of its biggest
accomplishments was the establishment of volunteer Task Forces charged
with the construction and maintenance of sections of the trail. Unfortu-

nately, by the late 1980s, the NCTA had become largely inactive, and it completely ceased operating in 1990. Thereafter, the MST languished for several years.

In an effort to revitalize MST efforts after the demise of the NCTA, Friends was formed in 1997 "to pursue the concept, research and provide information, advocate cooperative efforts among allied government offices and citizens, and support task forces and trail organizations for the benefit of a cross-state trail known as the Mountains to the Sea Trail."

In the twenty-plus years since its formation, Friends has helped the trail grow from a disjointed hodgepodge of trail sections totaling about 325 miles with ill-defined road connections to its current status as a complete, well-defined route across the state with over 700 miles of off-road trail. On average, Friends and its partners add about 15 miles of new trail each year.

In 2017, the MST took a step forward when the North Carolina legislature passed a bill officially making the Coastal Crescent Trail part of the MST. This route, an alternate to the originally proposed corridor along the Neuse River, was conceived and promoted by Friends. It strings together several areas of public lands, giving hikers opportunities to get off the roads for several significant stretches while work is underway to create a more complete off-road route. The coastal plain hikes presented in this book are on this route.

On September 9, 2017, to celebrate the fortieth anniversary of Howard Lee's speech proposing the MST, Friends organized "MST in a Day," a collaborative effort to hike and paddle the entire length of the trail in one day. On that day, over 1,700 people of all ages and abilities collectively traveled every mile of the MST; to the best of our knowledge, this was the first time such a feat has been accomplished on any long-distance trail anywhere.

REGIONS AND SEGMENTS

To make it easier for hikers to use the MST, Friends has divided the trail into three regions, corresponding to the state's geographic areas. The MST is further divided into eighteen segments, each highlighting a part of North Carolina with unique natural and historic features:

- The Mountain Region, Segments 1 through 5, including about 350 miles of trail, stretches from Clingmans Dome in Great Smoky Mountains National Park to Devils Garden Overlook on the Blue Ridge Parkway near Stone Mountain State Park and Sparta.
- The Piedmont Region, Segments 6 through 10, continues from

Devils Garden Overlook to Falls Lake dam near Raleigh, about 300 miles.

- The Coastal Plain and Outer Banks Region, Segments 11 through 18, covers about 525 miles, from Falls Lake dam to Jockey's Ridge State Park, and includes a paddle alternate along the Neuse River.

Appendix 1 lists the names and endpoints of each of the eighteen segments and the paddle alternate.

ALLOWABLE MODES OF TRAVEL

As a long-distance trail with varying trail types and different land managers, the MST has varying restrictions on what travel modes are allowed. Hiking is, of course, allowed anywhere on the MST. Other modes are allowed as follows:

- On all public roads, including dirt or sand roads, all modes of travel are allowed, including automobiles, bicycles, or walking.
- On greenways and other paved multiuse paths, cycling and hiking are allowed, but motorized vehicles generally are not.
- On beaches, bicycles are generally allowed, although there may be restrictions at certain times to protect wildlife. In addition, most of the beaches along the MST are fairly soft, and it may not be possible or pleasant to ride a bike on them. Portions of the beaches in the Cape Hatteras National Seashore are also open to off-road vehicles with a permit.
- Horses are prohibited on most of the MST but are allowed on a few sections. The only hikes in this book that include any trail open to horses are Hike 10, Cone Manor Carriage Trails: Shulls Mill Road to Flat Top Manor, and Hike 16, Hanging Rock State Park: Tory's Den parking lot to Hanging Rock Lake.
- Mountain biking is generally not allowed on the natural surface trails making up the MST, but there are a few exceptions. The only such exception included in this book is the Elkin & Alleghany Rail-Trail, part of Hike 14.

TRAIL MARKINGS

The official blaze of the MST is a 3-inch white circle. Nearly all of the off-road portions of the trail are well marked with this blaze. Some sections have kiosks or other markers providing additional guidance. Blue blazes identify many of the spur trails connecting the MST to roads.

Highway signs along many of the road portions of the MST identify them as the current route and provide wayfinding assistance. In addition, where possible, most road sections have white circle blazes, painted on the left shoulder in the hiker's direction of travel.

About Friends of the Mountains-to-Sea Trail

Friends of the Mountains-to-Sea Trail is a nonprofit organization that brings together communities and volunteers to support the MST. Its work focuses on four areas: (1) building and maintaining trail, (2) enhancing the trail route, (3) encouraging people to use the trail, and (4) expanding support.

Friends' trail building and maintenance efforts are led by its volunteer-based "Task Forces," which continue the tradition started by the NCTA. Each of these groups (there are currently twenty-three of them) is responsible for a specific trail section. Although coordinated through Friends, the Task Forces have significant autonomy. Indeed, several are separate nonprofits, including the Carolina Mountain Club, High Peaks Trail Association, Elkin Valley Trails Association, Sauratown Trails Association, Friends of the Sauratown Mountains, and Carteret County Wildlife Club.

Route enhancements include our work to improve the hiking experience—identifying and opening campsites, providing interesting routes on quiet back roads to connect sections of completed trail, recruiting "trail angels" who can help thru-hikers on their statewide treks. Additionally, we work with State Parks, local governments, and nonprofit land trusts to help them acquire more land to build new sections of trail.

To encourage people to use the MST, we spread the word about the trail to interested groups throughout the state and beyond, and we serve as the primary source of information about how to hike the trail—through our website (MountainstoSeaTrail.org) and our trail guides.

Finally, we expand support for the MST through our advocacy work, helping elected officials—local, state, and federal—and citizens understand the value of the trail for recreation, quality of life, the economy, and the environment. Just as important, we are a source of information for our governments to help them make the trail happen.

Building and maintaining trail, acquiring land, providing trail enhancements, and raising awareness and support are critical, ongoing jobs. You can get involved and help support the trail through Friends by emailing info@MountainstoSeaTrail.org; going online at MountainstoSeaTrail.org; calling 919-825-0297; or writing Friends of the MST, PO Box 10431, Raleigh, NC 27605.

About the Day Hikes

This guide presents forty day hikes carefully chosen from across the entire length of the MST, including two to three hikes from each of the eighteen MST segments. They do not necessarily represent secluded areas or hidden gems of the trail (although some are). Nor are they the most difficult portions (although a few will challenge most hikers), or even the most scenic parts of the trail (although there is no shortage of stunning beauty represented in these pages).

Instead, our goal in choosing these hikes is to capture North Carolina's great variety and diversity, from the mountains to the sea, from its past to its future, from wilderness to farmland to the city. We hope that a person who completes all the hikes in this book will encounter the entire North Carolina experience: its culture; its history; its landscapes, ecology, and geology; and its wonderful people.

The hikes presented in this book vary greatly in length, difficulty, and surroundings, but we have tried to make most of them accessible to hikers of average ability and fitness. In keeping with the linear nature of the MST, most of the hikes begin at one spot and end at another and can be completed either as out-and-back hikes or by setting a shuttle and hiking one-way. A few are loops or "lollipops" that return to the same place they begin. Nearly all of the hikes can be made shorter or longer simply by turning around before the end or by continuing past the trailhead described in the book. (Mile-by-mile instructions for the entire MST are available on the Friends website at MountainstoSeaTrail.org/the-trail/trail-guides.)

For simplicity, we have presented the directions for these hikes in one direction only. In general, we have chosen the direction we think best shows off the hike or, if that is not a material consideration, the direction an eastbound hiker from Clingmans Dome to Jockey's Ridge would walk. Of course, any of these hikes can be done in the opposite direction if preferred.

Our last hope is that the hikes in this book will inspire some readers to explore more of the MST and perhaps even become one of our trail completers. For more information and resources on completing a thru-hike or section hike of the MST, see Appendix 2: Completing the MST.

Seasonal Hiking

One of the great things about North Carolina is the opportunity for four-season hiking. Indeed, each season offers its own set of rewards. In winter, crowds are smaller, light snows can make for an enchanting white wonderland, and the bare trees open up views that are hidden in other seasons. Spring brings spectacular profusions of wildflowers, which can be enjoyed again and again simply by hiking at higher elevations through the season, and many people believe the many shades of green shown by early spring's new leaf growth, although subtler, create an even prettier palette than fall's leaf change. Summer's wild riot of plant growth reminds us how fertile the state is, and a trip to high elevation or a dip in one of our many swimming holes provides relief from the heat. Autumn justifiably brings "leaf-peepers" from all over the country to western North Carolina, but good fall color can be found anywhere in the state, and the cooler temperatures and drier air mean fewer insects and more pleasant hiking in our hotter regions.

With one exception, all of the hikes in this book can be hiked year-round, although, particularly in the mountains, winter weather can temporarily shut down access. Even the one exception, Hike 1 from Clingmans Dome, can be accessed by those willing to hike or bike on the closed Clingmans Dome Rd. or hike in on the Appalachian Trail, but distance and short daylight hours make this inadvisable for all but strong hikers.

On the other side of the spectrum, notoriously ferocious insects make several of the coastal-plain hikes unpleasant in summer, especially when combined with the high temperatures and humidity. We have noted the hikes where this is especially true.

Whatever the season, North Carolina's weather is notoriously volatile. When a storm rolls in, temperatures can drop dramatically, and what was a warm, sunny day can quickly become unpleasant or even life-threatening. On some of the highest peaks, snow has been reported every month of the year. Never head out on a hike without appropriate rain gear and warm clothing.

Disclaimer

Friends has tried to make this guide as accurate as possible and will up-date it regularly through the website's "Trail Updates" page, but trail con-ditions constantly change, and the guide may contain mistakes or out-dated information. If you do find inaccuracies in the book, please send corrections to info@MountainstoSeaTrail.org. Finally, please remember that this or any other guidebook is no substitute for good judgment, maps, and route-finding skills.

Conclusion

On the hikes in this book, you will experience North Carolina's wilder-ness, wildlife, small towns, farms, and historic sites. You will enjoy rivers, islands, lakes, bays, urban greenways, forests, mountains, and beaches. You will get a real feel for the sights, sounds, and people of North Carolina. We hope you'll join us on the MST to experience this slice of our beautiful state. Enjoy!

HOW TO USE THIS GUIDEBOOK

SELECTING A HIKE

This book includes several resources to help readers choose their hikes. First is the hike table (page 13), which identifies the length, difficulty, and MST segment of each hike. The hike finder (page 17) lists hikes that represent various attributes of the trail. The map on page 19 shows the locations of each of the hikes.

Once these resources have narrowed down the choices, the individual hike descriptions provide details to help you with the final decision. Before setting out on any of these hikes, though, check for any trail closures or other updates at MountainstoSeaTrail.org/updates.

HIKE DESCRIPTIONS

Each hike description contains the following elements:

HIKE SUMMARY

The information that begins each hike description summarizes the crucial information about the hike as follows.

Distance. As mentioned, most of the hikes in this book are point-to-point; in those cases, we provide both one-way and round-trip distances between the trailheads. For a few loops or "lollipops," or where logistical issues such as access restrictions require an out-and-back hike, we provide only the total distance.

Degree of difficulty. This is a subjective rating based on several factors including length, total elevation change, and the quality of the trail tread. In general, hikes are classified as shown below, although a few hikes vary because of individual considerations.

- Easy: less than 5 miles one-way and mostly flat; smooth or paved trail or road.
- Moderate: 3 to 5 miles one-way; some hills; some rocks or other obstacles on the trail.
- Strenuous: more than 5 miles one-way or more than 2,000 feet of elevation change; challenging trail tread.

Trail type. This states whether the hike is on roads, paved paths, or natural-surface trails. Although it is not a precise predictor of how busy or secluded the hike will be, it provides some indication.

Trailheads. This identifies each trailhead by name, describes any services or amenities available there, and lists the trailhead's GPS coordinates and elevation. For point-to-point hikes, "Trailhead 1" identifies the trailhead where the directions begin at mile 0.0.

Total elevation change. These figures are the cumulative totals of all the uphills and downhills on the hike (in the case of point-to-point hikes, going from Trailhead 1 to Trailhead 2). The total elevation change can be helpful in determining the difficulty of a hike, but keep in mind that the same elevation change over 5 miles will feel much less strenuous than if it were over only 1 mile.

MST segment. This section places the day hike within the overall MST, using Friends' eighteen segments, and can be useful to locate hikes or for hikers wanting to add more mileage by continuing past the day hike trailheads, using the segment guides available on Friends' website. We have not included specific mileages within segments, because they are subject to frequent change as sections of trail are added or rerouted, especially in the Piedmont and coastal plain. Most of the day hikes in this book can easily be located within the segment by using the primary parking table.

Highlights. This is a brief description of a few key reasons we have included the hike. In many but not all cases, these characteristics are also reflected in the Hike Finder.

Dogs. This tells whether dogs are allowed on the hike, along with any other restrictions, such as leash length.

HIKE OVERVIEW

The Hike Overview section provides details about highlights and points of interest along the hike, turns or other points that require special care, and similar information. It is designed to be used in conjunction with, but not as a substitute for, the Hike Directions.

DRIVING DIRECTIONS

Driving directions are provided from a single location (or, in a very few cases, two locations), typically a major highway or nearby town. From other locations, the route described may not be the best one. In some cases, we also provide directions for the shuttles between trailheads. See "GPS Information," later in this section, for more information about using GPS coordinates from the hike summary to find trailheads.

HIKE DIRECTIONS

This section provides turn-by-turn directions for the entire hike, to 0.1-mile precision. Keep in mind that side trips, detours, backtracking, and other factors mean that the actual distance walked by a hiker is rarely precisely the same as the trail distance.

SPECIAL CONSIDERATIONS

Any cautions or other logistical information specific to a hike are included in this section.

FOR MORE INFORMATION

This section lists additional websites, maps, books, or other resources for information about the hike.

MAP

Each hike includes a map showing the route, topography (except where the hike is very flat), access roads and trailheads, and landmarks or other noteworthy features along or near the trail.

SPECIAL NOTES ABOUT THE BLUE RIDGE PARKWAY

Many of the hikes in the mountain region are accessed by, or begin and end on, the Blue Ridge Parkway. Two factors regarding navigation on the parkway are worth noting.

First, all directions on the parkway are described as "North," going from Cherokee, NC, toward Virginia, or "South," going from Virginia toward Cherokee. Because the parkway twists and turns, these directions do not always correspond to actual on-the-ground directions. Indeed, someone driving "south" on the parkway may at times be driving due north. All major points of access to the parkway are well marked with signs indicating "North" and "South."

Second, the entire length of the parkway is marked with concrete mileposts showing the distance from the northern terminus in Virginia. These mileposts are on the right for a "southbound" traveler and are used to help locate landmarks and trailheads.

GPS INFORMATION

The hike summaries include GPS coordinates (latitude and longitude) for each of the trailheads. These coordinates can be entered just like a street address into mapping programs such as Google Maps or Apple Maps to provide directions to the trailheads. Cell service may not always be available, however, especially at some of the more remote mountain hike locations, which can restrict the ability to use these features.

There are several smartphone apps that allow maps, routes, and other GPS information to be downloaded over a cellular or Wi-Fi network and then used in the field even if cell service is not available. These apps rely on the phone's GPS radio, which does not require a cellular signal. Popular and well-regarded apps include MotionX-GPS (available only for iOS, not Android), BackCountry Navigator (Android only), and Gaia GPS (both). Popular fitness-tracking apps such as Strava, Ride with GPS, or MapMy-Hike may also provide offline capabilities. Most of these products require either a one-time purchase or a subscription to enable map and trail route downloads.

Downloadable GPX and KML files containing the route of each of the day hikes in this book are available on Friends' website at Mountainsto SeaTrail.org/day-hikes. Consult your app's or GPS device's documentation for instructions on installing and using these files.

When hiking in areas without cell service, using airplane mode can help save battery life. For most smartphones, airplane mode does not turn off the GPS radio, but confirm this on your phone before relying on it.

Stand-alone GPS units that do not require cell service are also available. These may provide more features and be more accurate than a smartphone, but they may be overkill for users who simply want to follow a trail.

HIKE TABLE

Hike	MST segment	One-way or loop distance	Difficulty
1. The Great Smokies: Clingmans Dome to Fork Ridge Trail	Segment 1	4.5 miles	Moderate
2. The Oconaluftee River Trail: Oconaluftee Visitor Center to the Blue Ridge Parkway	Segment 1	0.7 mile	Easy
3. The Balsams: Waterrock Knob to Fork Ridge Overlook	Segment 2	2.5 miles	Moderate
4. Graveyard Ridge and Skinny Dip Falls: Black Balsam Knob Road to Cherry Cove Overlook	Segment 2	6.8 miles	Strenuous
5. The Shut-In Trail: Pisgah Inn to Mills River Valley Overlook	Segment 3	4.5 miles	Moderate
6. Rattlesnake Lodge: Craven Gap to Tanbark Ridge Tunnel	Segment 3	4.4 miles	Moderate to strenuous
7. The Craggies: Glassmine Falls Overlook to Graybeard Overlook	Segment 3	2.3 miles	Moderate
8. Linville Gorge: Wolf Pit Road to Table Rock	Segment 4	8.4 miles	Strenuous
9. Waterfalls: Pineola Road to Roseboro Road	Segment 4	3.6 miles	Moderate but requires some wading
10. Cone Manor Carriage Trails: Shulls Mill Road to Flat Top Manor	Segment 5	4.3 miles	Moderate
11. The Blue Ridge Escarpment: Cascades Recreation Area to Benge Gap	Segment 5	4.1 miles	Moderate

Hike	MST segment	One-way or loop distance	Difficulty
12. The Bluff Mountain Trail: Basin Cove Overlook to Doughton Park Visitor Center	Segment 5	4.3 miles	Moderate
13. Stone Mountain State Park: Backpack Parking to Upper Trailhead Parking	Segment 6	5.0 miles	Strenuous
14. Elkin and the E&A Rail-Trail: Downtown Elkin to US 21 at Collins Road	Segment 6	3.3 miles	Easy
15. Pilot Mountain Loop	Segment 7	6.3 miles	Moderate
16. Hanging Rock State Park: Tory's Den Parking Lot to Hanging Rock Lake	Segment 7	5.3 miles	Moderate to strenuous
17. Cascades Preserve Loop	Segment 8	2.0 miles	Easy
18. Greensboro Watershed Lakes: Lake Brandt Marina to Church Street	Segment 8	3.5 miles	Easy to moderate
19. The Haw River Trail: Great Bend Park to Stoney Creek Marina	Segment 9	2.9 miles	Moderate
20. Hillsborough's Riverwalk: Gold Park to Occoneechee Speedway	Segment 9	2.1 miles	Easy
21. The Eno River: Cabe Lands to Pump Station	Segment 10	1.7 to 4.4 miles	Moderate
22. The Falls Lake Trail: Rolling View State Recreation Area to Little Lick Creek	Segment 10	4.5 miles	Moderate
23. Fall Line Geology: Raven Ridge Road to Falls Lake Dam Spillway	Segment 10	3.5 miles	Moderate

Hike	MST segment	One-way or loop distance	Difficulty
24. Raleigh's Neuse River Greenway: Buffaloe Road to Milburnie Park	Segment 11	4.4 miles	Easy
25. Smithfield's Neuse Riverwalk: Smithfield Recreation and Aquatics Center to Bob Wallace Jaycee Kiddie Park	Segment 11	3.1 miles	Easy
26. Bentonville Battlefield: Harper House to Cole Plantation	Segment 12	2.3 miles	Easy
27. Downtown Roseboro Loop	Segment 12	1.9 miles	Easy
28. Old Cape Fear Countryside: White Oak Post Office to Harmony Hall	Segment 13	2.1 miles	Easy
29. Turnbull Creek and Jones Lake: Turnbull Creek Educational State Forest Office to Jones Lake State Park Visitor Center	Segment 13	1.0 mile	Easy
30. Moores Creek National Battlefield Loop	Segment 14	0.9 mile	Easy
31. Burgaw Greenway Loop	Segment 14	2.7 miles	Easy
32. Stones Creek Game Land: NC 210 to US 17	Segment 15	3.5 miles	Moderate
33. Lejeune Memorial Greenway: Montford Point Road to Holcomb Boulevard	Segment 15	Variable, up to 4.8 miles	Easy to moderate
34. The Northern Neusiok Trail: NC 101 to Billfinger Road	Segment 16	3.3 miles	Moderate
35. The Southern Neusiok Trail: Oyster Point Loop	Segments 16 and 17	2.8 miles	Easy

Hike	MST segment	One-way or loop distance	Difficulty
36. "Down East" North Carolina: Williston to Davis	Segment 17	3.9 miles	Easy
37. Cedar Island National Wildlife Refuge: Cedar Island High Bridge to Cedar Island Volunteer Fire Department	Segment 17	5.9 miles	Easy to moderate
38. Cape Hatteras: Hatteras Lighthouse to Frisco Campground	Segment 18	5.7 miles	Moderate to strenuous
39. Outer Banks Wildlife and Beaches: Pea Island National Wildlife Refuge Headquarters to Marc Basnight Bridge	Segment 18	5.4 miles	Easy to moderate
40. Jockey's Ridge State Park	Segment 18	0.5 mile	Easy

HIKE FINDER

To help with hike planning, we have grouped together some of our favorite hikes in several different categories. Use these lists together with the location map and hike summary tables to find the most suitable hike for you.

Favorite hikes for . . .

BIRDING AND WILDLIFE

2. The Oconaluftee River Trail
5. The Shut-In Trail
30. Moores Creek National Battlefield Loop
35. The Southern Neusiok Trail
37. Cedar Island National Wildlife Refuge
39. Outer Banks Wildlife and Beaches

HISTORY BUFFS

5. The Shut-In Trail
6. Rattlesnake Lodge
10. Cone Manor Carriage Trails
14. Elkin and the E&A Rail-Trail
19. The Haw River Trail
20. Hillsborough's Riverwalk
24. Raleigh's Neuse River Greenway
26. Bentonville Battlefield
27. Downtown Roseboro Loop
28. Old Cape Fear Countryside
30. Moores Creek National Battlefield Loop

UNIQUE ECOLOGY OR GEOLOGY

1. The Great Smokies
11. The Blue Ridge Escarpment
13. Stone Mountain State Park
15. Pilot Mountain Loop
23. Fall Line Geology
29. Turnbull Creek and Jones Lake
40. Jockey's Ridge State Park

WATERFALLS

4. Graveyard Ridge and Skinny Dip Falls
9. Waterfalls
11. The Blue Ridge Escarpment

13. Stone Mountain State Park

17. Cascades Preserve Loop

WILDFLOWERS

2. The Oconaluftee River Trail

6. Rattlesnake Lodge

7. The Craggies

12. The Bluff Mountain Trail

17. Cascades Preserve Loop

18. Greensboro Watershed Lakes

21. The Eno River

NORTH CAROLINA'S SMALL TOWNS

14. Elkin and the E&A Rail-Trail

20. Hillsborough's Riverwalk

27. Downtown Roseboro Loop

31. Burgaw Greenway Loop

36. "Down East" North Carolina

WATER LOVERS

2. The Oconaluftee River Trail

9. Waterfalls

16. Hanging Rock State Park

18. Greensboro Watershed Lakes

19. The Haw River Trail

21. The Eno River

SUMMER COOLDOWN

1. The Great Smokies

5. The Shut-In Trail

10. Cone Manor Carriage Trails

15. Pilot Mountain Loop

16. Hanging Rock State Park

UNIVERSAL ACCESSIBILITY

2. The Oconaluftee River Trail

20. Hillsborough's Riverwalk

24. Raleigh's Neuse River Greenway

25. Smithfield's Neuse Riverwalk

27. Downtown Roseboro Loop

30. Moores Creek National Battlefield Loop

31. Burgaw Greenway Loop

33. Lejeune Memorial Greenway

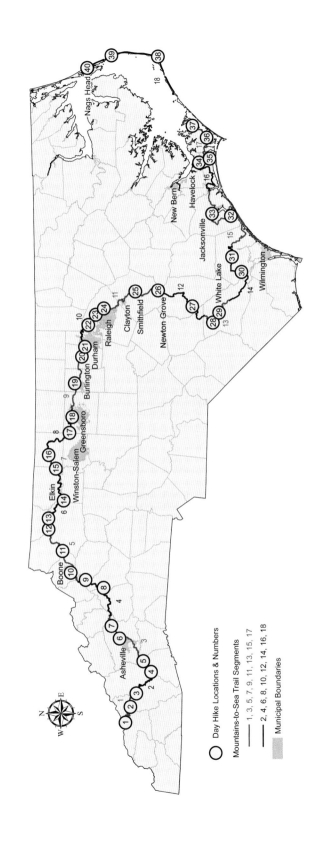

Nags Head

New Bern

Havelock

Jacksonville

White Lake

Wilmington

Clayton

Smithfield

Newton Grove

Raleigh

Durham

Burlington

Greensboro

Winston-Salem

Elkin

Boone

Asheville

Day Hike Locations & Numbers

Mountains-to-Sea Trail Segments
1, 3, 5, 7, 9, 11, 13, 15, 17
2, 4, 6, 8, 10, 12, 14, 16, 18
Municipal Boundaries

Day Hike Map Legend

——— Day Hike	——— Major contour interval
——— Mountains-to-Sea Trail	········ Minor contour interval
══◆══ Interstates	——— Rivers / creeks
═◯═ US highways	▓▓▓ Water bodies
═◯═ NC highways	▒▒▒ Parks
——— Local roads	▨▨▨ Military installation
┌┄┄┐ State boundary	● Unincorporated Place

🚶	Day hike termini	▯	Lighthouse
▬	Bridge	▲	Mountain
✚	Cemetery	▯	Point of interest
◪	Dam	⊞	Picnic area
⛴	Ferry	🚶	Trailhead
🏛	Historic site	▯	Visitor center
◘	Historic house	◪	Waterfall

Mountain Region

Hike 1

THE GREAT SMOKIES *Clingmans Dome to Fork Ridge Trail*

Sunrise from Clingmans Dome. Photo by Christine Hoyer.

Distance: 4.5 miles one-way (3.9 miles on MST plus 0.6-mile spur to parking); 9.0 miles round-trip

Degree of difficulty: Moderate

Trail type: Paved and natural-surface trail

Trailhead 1: Clingmans Dome parking lot; restrooms

Trailhead 1 coordinates: N35.55674, W83.49618

Trailhead 1 elevation: 6,288 feet

Trailhead 2: Fork Ridge Trailhead; no facilities

Trailhead 2 coordinates: N35.59031, W83.46946

Trailhead 2 elevation: 5,881 feet

Total elevation change: gain, 966 feet; loss, 1,373 feet

MST segment: 1

Highlights: Western terminus of MST; highest point in the Smokies; high-elevation spruce-fir forest; outstanding views

Dogs: Not allowed

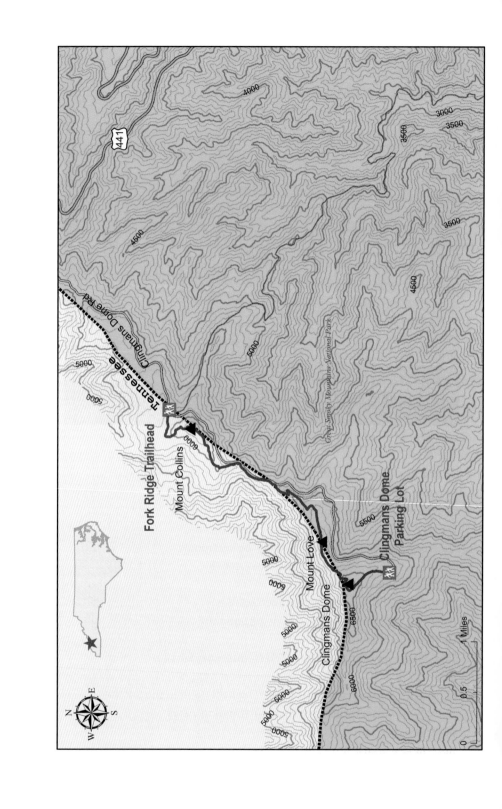

HIKE OVERVIEW

Although this hike begins at one of the busiest areas in Great Smoky Mountains National Park (GSMNP), it quickly leaves the crowds behind for a wonderful high-elevation experience. From the Clingmans Dome parking lot, the hike begins on a paved, 0.6-mile trail to the summit, not officially part of the MST. Along the way, an information station and store managed by the Great Smoky Mountains Association (open every day April–November; hours vary) is a good place to find more information about the area.

At 6,643 feet, Clingmans Dome is the highest point in GSMNP and Tennessee (it is on the NC-TN border), and the third-highest summit east of the Mississippi. Clingmans Dome also has special significance to Friends of the MST, because this is "where it all begins"—the westernmost point of the trail. (Hike 40, Jockey's Ridge State Park, includes the corresponding eastern end.)

At the summit, be sure to walk up the observation tower, where on a clear day you can see seven states. Returning to the trail, follow the signs for the Mountains-to-Sea Trail and the Appalachian Trail, which runs concurrently with the MST for this entire hike.

For the next 4 miles, the trail passes through a high-elevation spruce-fir forest, a forest type more commonly associated with Canada than with North Carolina. The dominant tree species here are red spruce and Fraser fir. Unfortunately, many of the trees have been killed by the balsam woolly adelgid, a parasitic insect introduced from Europe.

The trail stays at or near the ridgeline to cross Mt. Love (6,411 feet), Collins Gap, and the summit of Mt. Collins (6,188 feet). None of these is particularly prominent, but they are noted on maps. Just before the summit of Mt. Collins, there is a nice resting spot with flat rocks and views to the southeast on the right. At 4.2 miles, the Sugarland Mountain Trail comes in on the left, and 0.3 mile farther, a spur trail on the right, marked with a sign for Fork Ridge Trail, leads a short distance to Clingmans Dome Rd., the Fork Ridge Trailhead, and the end of the hike.

DRIVING DIRECTIONS

To reach the trailheads, take US 441 west from Cherokee or east from Gatlinburg. At Newfound Gap, the NC/TN line, turn onto Clingmans Dome Rd. The Fork Ridge Trailhead is 3.5 miles ahead on the left. Continue another 3.5 miles to the end of the road to reach the Clingmans Dome parking lot.

HIKE DIRECTIONS

0.0 From the upper end of the Clingmans Dome parking lot, walk up the paved path leading to the observation tower.

0.6 Just before the ramp to the observation tower, turn left at a sign marked "Appalachian Trail/Mountains-to-Sea Trail." After about 100 feet, turn right at the MST sign.

1.2 Continue straight over summit of Mt. Love (6,411 feet).

2.6 Continue straight at Collins Gap.

3.6 Continue straight to ascend the summit of Mt. Collins.

4.2 Continue straight through the intersection with Sugarland Mountain Trail.

4.5 Turn right on a spur trail marked for the Fork Ridge Trail and continue 125 feet to the end of the hike at the Fork Ridge Trailhead on Clingmans Dome Rd.

SPECIAL CONSIDERATIONS

Clingmans Dome Rd. is closed December 1 to March 31 and when weather conditions require.

Temperatures at the summit of Clingmans Dome can be 10–20 degrees Fahrenheit lower than in the surrounding lowlands. Be prepared for any kind of weather, even in the summer.

FOR MORE INFORMATION

GSMNP: www.nps.gov/grsm

GSMNP Trail Map: www.nps.gov/grsm/planyourvisit/upload/GSMNP-Map_JUNE14-complete4-2.pdf

GSMNP seasonal road closures: www.nps.gov/grsm/planyourvisit/seasonalroads.htm

Other GSMNP road closures: www.nps.gov/grsm/planyourvisit/temproadclose.htm or twitter.com/SmokiesRoadsNPS

Carolina Mountain Club website (trail maintainers in this segment): www.carolinamountainclub.org

Walt Weber and "the Gang" for the Carolina Mountain Club, *Trail Profiles and Maps: From Clingmans Dome to Mount Mitchell and Beyond* (3rd ed. 2018), has detailed elevation profiles and maps for Segments 1–3 of the MST, as well as historical information about several of the areas covered in this book.

Hike 2

THE OCONALUFTEE RIVER TRAIL

Oconaluftee Visitor Center to the Blue Ridge Parkway

Oconaluftee elk standoff. Photo by Nancy Wilson.

Distance: 0.7 mile one-way; 1.4 miles round-trip
Degree of difficulty: Easy
Trail type: Natural-surface trail
Trailhead 1: Oconaluftee Visitor Center; water, restrooms, supplies
Trailhead 1 coordinates: N35.51334, W83.30614
Trailhead 1 elevation: 2,041 feet
Trailhead 2: US 441/Blue Ridge Parkway Junction; no facilities
Trailhead 2 coordinates: N35.50567, W83.30079
Trailhead 2 elevation: 2,034 feet
Total elevation change: gain, 0 feet; loss, 7 feet
MST segment: 1
Highlights: Historic pioneer farmstead exhibit; Cherokee culture; river views; wildflowers; wildlife
Dogs: Allowed on leash

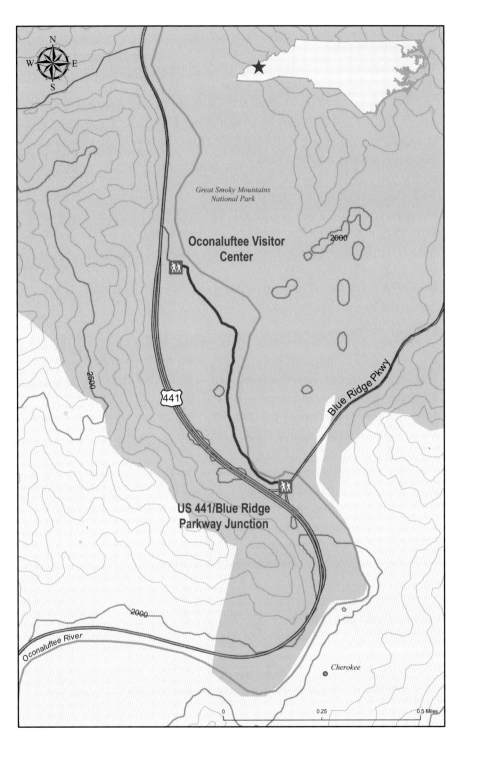

Great Smoky Mountains
National Park

Oconaluftee Visitor
Center

2000

2600

441

Blue Ridge Pkwy

US 441/Blue Ridge
Parkway Junction

2000

Oconaluftee River

Cherokee

0   0.25   0.5 Miles

HIKE OVERVIEW

This short hike, with a flat and level tread, offers an easy introduction to the natural and cultural history of Great Smoky Mountains National Park. The hike begins at GSMNP's Oconaluftee Visitor Center, open every day except Christmas; hours vary by season. A quick stop at the educational displays and store before starting the hike is worthwhile. Cold drinks and restrooms are also available here.

The route passes between the visitor center and restrooms on the sidewalk, then follows signs for the Oconaluftee River Trail onto a gravel path. The gravel path continues along a split-rail fence enclosing the Mountain Farm Museum. This replica mountain farmstead features buildings collected from locations throughout the park, including a log farmhouse, a barn, an apple house, a springhouse, and a working blacksmith shop. Most were built in the late nineteenth century and moved to the present location in the 1950s. The site also showcases historic gardening and agricultural practices.

At the end of the fence enclosing the museum, the trail turns right, into the woods, and travels downstream along the Oconaluftee, a shallow, relatively broad river. The forest here is known for the number and variety of wildflowers, and there are several display panels illustrating the historical uses of the river by the Cherokee. Keep an eye out for elk, which frequent the river and nearby fields. A large variety of wildflowers bloom in profusion all along the trail, especially in spring.

Just before the first road bridge, a side trail on the right leads to a small parking pullout at the intersection of the Blue Ridge Parkway (BRP) and US 441, the end of this hike. There are actually two side trails, and either one will take you to Trailhead 2. If you want to keep walking, the MST continues across the bridge along the BRP, while the Oconaluftee River Trail continues straight about another mile into the town of Cherokee.

DRIVING DIRECTIONS

From Cherokee, NC, head toward GSMNP on US 441 (Cherokee's main road). Approximately 0.4 mile past the large sign marking the entrance to the park, the BRP intersects from the right. The small gravel pullout here is Trailhead 2. Continue another 0.6 mile to the Oconaluftee Visitor Center, Trailhead 1.

HIKE DIRECTIONS

0.0 From the parking lot, walk on the sidewalk between the Oconaluftee Visitor Center and restrooms. At a fork in the sidewalk, take the right fork, signed to Oconaluftee River Trail. At a second Oconaluftee River Trail sign, continue onto the gravel path, passing alongside a split-rail fence.

0.2 At the end of the fence, turn right to follow the Oconaluftee River Trail.

0.7 Turn right on a side trail just before a road bridge, then reach the intersection of US 441 and the BRP, the end of the hike.

SPECIAL CONSIDERATIONS

The Oconaluftee Visitor Center is one of the busiest places in GSMNP. Even though the parking lot is large, it can fill up on a sunny summer weekend or when elk are present.

FOR MORE INFORMATION

GSMNP: www.nps.gov/grsm

GSMNP Trail Map: www.nps.gov/grsm/planyourvisit/upload/GSMNP -Map_JUNE14-complete4-2.pdf

GSMNP seasonal road closures: www.nps.gov/grsm/planyourvisit /seasonalroads.htm

Other GSMNP road closures: www.nps.gov/grsm/planyourvisit /temproadclose.htm or twitter.com/SmokiesRoadsNPS

BRP: www.nps.gov/blri

BRP road closures: www.nps.gov/blri/planyourvisit/roadclosures.htm

Carolina Mountain Club website (trail maintainers in this segment): www.carolinamountainclub.org

Walt Weber and "the Gang" for the Carolina Mountain Club, *Trail Profiles and Maps: From Clingmans Dome to Mount Mitchell and Beyond* (3rd ed. 2018), has detailed elevation profiles and maps for Segments 1–3 of the MST, as well as historical information about several of the areas covered in this book.

Hike 3

THE BALSAMS *Waterrock Knob to Fork Ridge Overlook*

A foggy day near Waterrock Knob. Photo by Jim Grode.

Distance: 2.5 miles one-way; 5.0 miles round-trip
Degree of difficulty: Moderate
Trail type: Natural-surface trail
Trailhead 1: Waterrock Knob Visitor Center (BRP MP 451.2); supplies, restrooms
Trailhead 1 coordinates: N35.46010, W83.14048
Trailhead 1 elevation: 5,812 feet
Trailhead 2: Fork Ridge Overlook (BRP MP 449.0); no facilities
Trailhead 2 coordinates: N35.45936, W83.11681
Trailhead 2 elevation: 5,266 feet
Total elevation change: gain, 656 feet; loss, 1,202 feet
MST segment: 2
Highlights: Great views; moderate hike in challenging landscape; diverse flora and fauna
Dogs: Allowed on leash

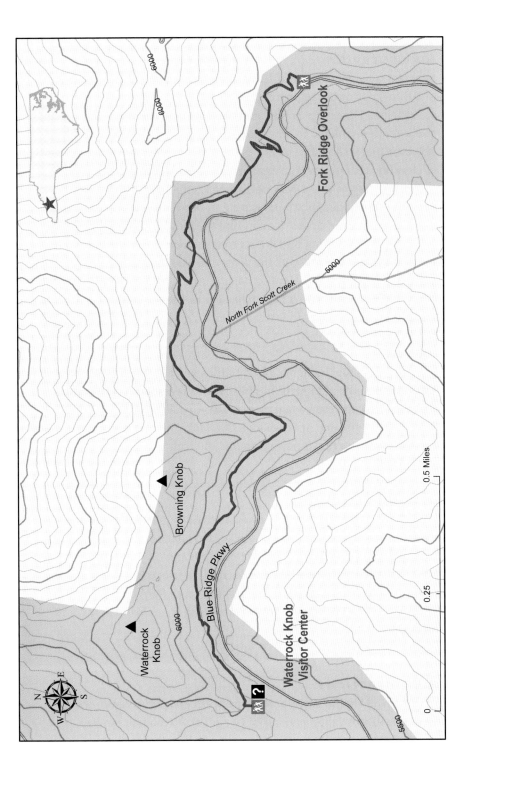

HIKE OVERVIEW

Segment 2 is one of the most challenging segments of the entire MST, and this is one of the segment's few areas that is easily accessible to the casual hiker. The access points are close together, and the grade is relatively gentle compared to other parts of Segment 2. That does not mean, however, that it should be taken lightly; there is still a reasonable amount of elevation change, and the weather can be very unpredictable.

The hike begins at the Waterrock Knob Visitor Center, with a small convenience store (open 9:00 A.M.–5:00 P.M. between April and November; early in the season, closed Tuesday and Wednesday) and restrooms, but no water. Before setting out, if it's a clear day, check out the information panels that identify many of the distant peaks. The route heads up the paved trail from the back right corner of the parking area. After just a few yards, it turns right onto a trail marked with the MST blaze. Continuing straight up the paved path instead leads 0.5 mile to the 6,292-foot summit of Waterrock Knob, which has even more spectacular views than the overlook.

The trail passes through high-altitude mixed hardwood and spruce-fir forest for the entire length of this hike, with a few small stream crossings that are often dry (even when there is water, your feet won't get wet) before reaching the end at Fork Ridge Overlook. The trail tread is rocky in places, but the footing is never extremely difficult.

DRIVING DIRECTIONS

From Waynesville, NC, take US 74 west to the BRP junction at Balsam Gap, approximately 7 miles from Waynesville, and head south on the parkway. After 5.4 miles, the Fork Ridge Overlook (MP 449.0), Trailhead 2 for this hike, is on the left. To reach Trailhead 1, the Waterrock Knob Visitor Center, continue another 2.2 miles on the BRP, then turn right on the Waterrock Knob access road (MP 451.2). Trailhead parking is approximately 0.2 mile ahead.

HIKE DIRECTIONS

0.0 Begin hiking the paved path at the upper end of the Waterrock Knob Visitor Center parking lot (MP 451.2). After about 150 feet, turn right from the paved path onto a trail marked with the MST blaze. (Continue straight up the paved path to reach the summit of Waterrock Knob in 0.5 mile.)

0.2   Cross a small streambed that is often dry. Over the next 2 miles, there are several such crossings.

0.3   Ascend a set of wooden steps.

1.1   Descend a set of rock steps.

2.4   Pass a fence on the right with views of Fork Ridge Overlook.

2.5   Descend a short set of wooden steps and begin walking along the North Fork of Scott Creek, more easily heard than seen from the trail, then reach the BRP at Fork Ridge Overlook (MP 449.0) to complete the hike.

SPECIAL CONSIDERATIONS

The BRP is often closed during the winter or in inclement weather, making access to this hike difficult or impossible. If you are unsure whether the parkway is open, check the National Park Service's "Blue Ridge Parkway Road Closure Map" (www.nps.gov/blri/planyourvisit/roadclosures.htm) for real-time closure information.

FOR MORE INFORMATION

BRP: www.nps.gov/blri

BRP Maps: www.nps.gov/blri/planyourvisit/maps.htm

Carolina Mountain Club website (trail maintainers in this segment): www.carolinamountainclub.org

Walt Weber and "the Gang" for the Carolina Mountain Club, *Trail Profiles and Maps: From Clingmans Dome to Mount Mitchell and Beyond* (3rd ed. 2018), has detailed elevation profiles and maps for Segments 1–3 of the MST, as well as historical information about several of the areas covered in this book.

Hike 4

GRAVEYARD RIDGE AND SKINNY DIP FALLS

Black Balsam Knob Road to Cherry Cove Overlook

Skinny Dip Falls.
Photo by Jim Grode.

Distance: 6.8 miles one-way; 13.6 miles round-trip
Degree of difficulty: Strenuous
Trail type: Natural-surface trail
Trailhead 1: Black Balsam Knob Rd. parking area (near BRP MP 420.2);
   no facilities
Trailhead 1 coordinates: N35.32066, W82.87616
Trailhead 1 elevation: 5,893 feet
Trailhead 2: Cherry Cove Overlook (BRP MP 415.7); no facilities
Trailhead 2 coordinates: N35.33582, W82.81537
Trailhead 2 elevation: 4,318 feet
Total elevation change: gain, 1,356 feet; loss, 2,927 feet
MST segment: 2
Highlights: Views; waterfalls; interesting natural history; high-elevation
   forest ecosystem
Dogs: Allowed on leash

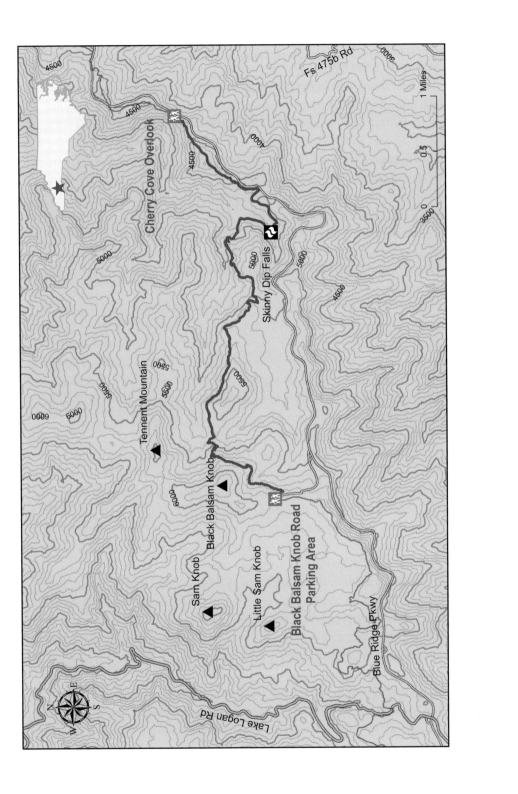

Cherry Cove Overlook

Fs 475b Rd

4500

4500

4500

4000

4500

4000

5000

5000

Skinny Dip Falls

5000

4500

5000

3500

3500

1 Miles

0.5

0

5000

5500

5500

5600

5500

Tennent Mountain

6000

6000

5600

6000

Sam Knob

Black Balsam Knob

Little Sam Knob

Black Balsam Knob Road
Parking Area

Blue Ridge Pkwy

Lake Logan Rd

N
E
W
S

HIKE OVERVIEW

The section of trail covered on this hike begins and ends near some of the most popular areas on the BRP. The 6,214-foot-high summit of nearby Black Balsam Knob is renowned for its views, and hundreds of people may walk up it on a warm sunny day. Just southeast, the parking lot for Graveyard Fields regularly overflows with walkers seeking a short, flat meadow hike complete with waterfalls. And the eastern end offers hikers and swimmers the short way in to Skinny Dip Falls, a spectacular (if not very high) waterfall and swimming hole.

Just a short distance from these attractions, though, the MST follows its own secluded route. This hike offers the same views, meadows, spring flowers, and fall leaves, and the waterfall, with only a fraction of the people.

For the first mile or so, the trail is fairly level. After a short but steep descent, it reaches a saddle with a major trail intersection at mile 1.6. Descending to the saddle at the upper reaches of the Yellowstone Prong, a small tributary of the Pigeon River, gives a sense of how Graveyard Fields got its name—the dead standing trees resulting from an early-twentieth-century blowdown were said to resemble so many gravestones. Although most of the dead trees are now gone, enough remain to conjure up the image, and the name endures.

From the saddle, the MST skirts the northern side of Graveyard Ridge, on the opposite side from the hustle and bustle of Graveyard Fields. The north side of the ridge may be less renowned, but it is no less beautiful, with high-altitude forest and occasional views into the Shining Rock Wilderness. Climbing back over the ridge, the MST returns to Graveyard Fields, where a side trail leads to Second Falls and then to the Graveyard Fields parking lot (MP 418.8) 0.4 mile away.

At mile 5.0, the trail crosses a bridge over the Yellowstone Prong, just below Skinny Dip Falls. This 30-foot-high, three-tiered waterfall and swimming hole is often crowded, but is well worth the visit. Despite the name, Skinny Dip Falls is not clothing-optional, but if the weather allows, bring swimwear and join in the fun!

A trail on the right at mile 5.3 leads 400 feet to parking at the Looking Glass Rock Overlook (MP 417.0). This side trail offers an option to reduce the hike distance by about 1.3 miles. The MST continues to parallel the BRP on or near the ridgetop to Cherry Cove Overlook (MP 415.7), the end of the hike.

DRIVING DIRECTIONS

From Asheville, head south on the BRP approximately 22 miles from the French Broad River crossing. Trailhead 2 is on the left at Cherry Cove Overlook (MP 415.7). Continue another 4.5 miles on the BRP to MP 420.2 and turn right on Forest Road 816, also known as Black Balsam Knob Rd. Travel about 0.7 mile up this road to reach on-road parking and the MST crossing at Trailhead 1.

HIKE DIRECTIONS

0.0 From the parking area, head east (right when facing away from the BRP) on the MST. Turn right just before the Art Loeb Trail sign. (Straight ahead is the trail up Black Balsam Knob.) Almost immediately, at a Y-intersection where the more obvious trail goes left, bear right into a spruce forest, following the white MST blazes.

0.1 In the next 0.4 mile, cross a series of thirteen wooden bridges and boardwalks over a network of streams.

0.4 Bear right at the top of a rock outcropping.

0.6 Begin descending a series of switchbacks.

0.9 Reach a clearing with a significant trail intersection and campsite. Continue straight, following the MST blaze and sign toward "BRP MP 417 Looking Glass Overlook."

1.6 Continue straight past the Graveyard Ridge Trail on the right.

3.3 Turn left at a T-intersection with another sign to "BRP MP 417 Looking Glass Overlook." *Note*: Turning right here leads to waterfalls and then the Graveyard Fields parking lot (MP 418.8) about 0.4 mile away.

3.6 Bear left at a Y-intersection where the right fork is marked for campsites.

5.0 Cross a wooden bridge over Yellowstone Prong just below Skinny Dip Falls, then ascend some stairs and cross a small stream on a wooden bridge.

5.3 Pass a side trail on the right to parking at the Looking Glass Rock Overlook 400 feet away (MP 417).

5.6 Turn right where Bridges Camp Gap Trail continues straight ahead.

6.8 Reach the end of the hike at Cherry Cove Overlook on the BRP (MP 415.7).

SPECIAL CONSIDERATIONS

As noted, this hike is in an extremely popular area. Parking can fill up quickly on a sunny summer weekend, so arrive early to be sure of getting a space.

The BRP is often closed during the winter or in inclement weather, making access to this hike difficult or impossible. If you are unsure whether the parkway is open, check the National Park Service's "Blue Ridge Parkway Road Closure Map" (www.nps.gov/blri/planyourvisit/roadclosures.htm) for real-time closure information.

FOR MORE INFORMATION

BRP: www.nps.gov/blri

BRP Maps: www.nps.gov/blri/planyourvisit/maps.htm

National Geographic Map 780 (Pisgah Ranger District): www.natgeo maps.com/ti_780

Carolina Mountain Club website (trail maintainers in this segment): www.carolinamountainclub.org

Walt Weber and "the Gang" for the Carolina Mountain Club, *Trail Profiles and Maps: From Clingmans Dome to Mount Mitchell and Beyond* (3rd ed. 2018), has detailed elevation profiles and maps for Segments 1–3 of the MST, as well as historical information about several of the areas covered in this book.

Hike 5

THE SHUT-IN TRAIL

Pisgah Inn to Mills River Valley Overlook

Buck Spring area in the snow.
Photo by Paul Malcolm.

Distance: 4.5 miles one-way; 9.0 miles round-trip
Degree of difficulty: Moderate
Trail type: Natural-surface trail
Trailhead 1: Pisgah Inn (BRP MP 406.8); food, supplies, water
Trailhead 1 coordinates: N35.40323, W82.75365
Trailhead 1 elevation: 4,921 feet
Trailhead 2: Mills River Valley Overlook (BRP MP 404.5); no facilities
Trailhead 2 coordinates: N35.44266, W82.71982
Trailhead 2 elevation: 4,081 feet
Total elevation change: gain, 1,116 feet; loss, 1,956 feet
MST segment: 3
Highlights: Views; history at Buck Spring Lodge ruins; relatively
  moderate grade for this area; birding
Dogs: Allowed on leash

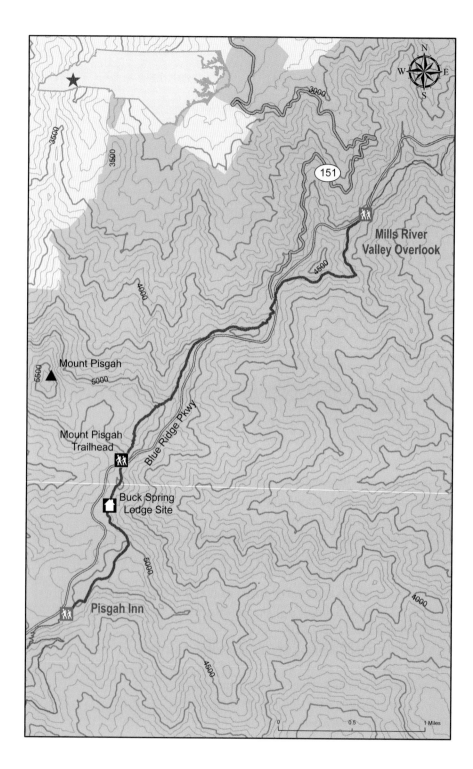

HIKE OVERVIEW

This hike begins at the back left corner (facing the inn) of the Pisgah Inn parking lot. The Pisgah Inn, open seasonally, has lodging, a well-known restaurant, and a store with general supplies. It is also famous for the views from its back terrace, which are worth a detour.

To begin the hike, find the kiosk for the Mt. Pisgah Trail System and MST signpost, and head up the stone stairs onto the trail. For the next mile, the trail traverses typical southern Appalachian hardwood forest, passing occasional overlooks and trail junctions.

At mile 1.0 is a clearing with wooden benches on the right. This is the former site of Buck Spring Lodge. This hunting lodge, built between 1896 and 1903 and later expanded, was George Vanderbilt's second house on his Biltmore Estate. Some of the ruins of the lodge and its outbuildings are still visible. The Carolina Mountain Club's *Trail Profiles and Maps* (see "For More Information" below) contains a wealth of historical information about the lodge and describes a tour of the area.

As it continues, the MST is also known as the Shut-In Trail. From here to the French Broad River, it follows the general route of the bridle trail Vanderbilt built to access the Buck Spring Lodge—occasionally on the old roadbed itself. Every fall this trail hosts the "Shut-In Ridge Trail Race," a grueling 17.8-mile run that attracts some of the best trail runners in the country.

At mile 1.4, the trail reaches the access road and parking area for the Mt. Pisgah trailhead. Here a side trail leads to the summit of Mt. Pisgah. Standing alone at 5,722 feet, its iconic pyramidal shape and the large communications tower on the summit make it instantly recognizable from its many vantage points throughout the region. The 2.3-mile (round-trip) trail to the summit can become extremely crowded but is rewarding.

The MST continues through mixed-hardwood forests, coming out one more time to the BRP at its junction with NC 151, before reaching the Mills River Valley Overlook and the end of the hike.

There is excellent birding in many places along this hike (see "For More Information" for a link to the North Carolina Birding Trail description). The Mills River Valley Overlook deserves special mention, however, as it is one of the best places to spot migrating hawks in mid- to late September.

DRIVING DIRECTIONS

From Asheville, drive south on the BRP approximately 11 miles from the French Broad River crossing. The Mills River Valley Overlook, Trailhead 2, is on the left at MP 404.5. Continue another 4.1 miles to Trailhead 1, the Pisgah Inn (MP 408.6).

HIKE DIRECTIONS

0.0 Begin the hike at the parking lot for the Pisgah Inn. Go to the back left corner of the parking lot (as viewed from the BRP), then go up the stone stairs at the MST signpost and kiosk for the Mt. Pisgah Trail System.

0.3 Continue straight past a side trail on the right leading to an overlook.

0.7 Continue straight past the junction with the Pilot Rock Trail on the right.

0.8 Continue straight past the junction with the Laurel Mountain Trail on the right.

1.0 Continue through a clearing at the former site of George Vanderbilt's Buck Spring Lodge, with wooden benches on the right and a spectacular view.

1.2 Continue straight across the parking area at Buck Springs Gap Overlook (MP 407.6).

1.4 Reach a road at the parking area for Mt. Pisgah trailhead (to your left) and walk along the shoulder, then return to the trail at stairs and a sign for "Shut-In Trail." *Note*: At this parking area (also at MP 407.6 but a little farther along the spur road than Buck Springs Gap Overlook), the trail crosses directly over the BRP's Buck Spring Tunnel, so the next time it reaches the BRP, it will be from the other side.

3.2 Reach the BRP at its junction with NC 151 and turn left to walk along the shoulder for approximately 75 yards, then cross the BRP and return to the trail at a white-blazed signpost. There is a small gravel parking area at this junction (MP 405.5).

4.5 Reach the Mills River Valley Overlook and the end of the hike.

SPECIAL CONSIDERATIONS

The BRP is often closed during the winter or in inclement weather, making access to this hike difficult or impossible. If you are unsure whether the parkway is open, check the National Park Service's "Blue Ridge Parkway Road Closure Map" (www.nps.gov/blri/planyourvisit/roadclosures.htm) for real-time closure information.

FOR MORE INFORMATION

BRP: www.nps.gov/blri

BRP Maps: www.nps.gov/blri/planyourvisit/maps.htm

Pisgah Inn website: www.pisgahinn.com

Carolina Mountain Club website (trail maintainers in this segment): www.carolinamountainclub.org

North Carolina Birding Trail: ncbirdingtrail.org/sites/2012/8/1/pisgah -ridge.html

Walt Weber and "the Gang" for the Carolina Mountain Club, *Trail Profiles and Maps: From Clingmans Dome to Mount Mitchell and Beyond* (3rd ed. 2018), has detailed elevation profiles and maps for Segments 1–3 of the MST, as well as historical information about several of the areas covered in this book.

Hike 6

RATTLESNAKE LODGE

Craven Gap to Tanbark Ridge Tunnel

Wild geranium and ruins at Rattlesnake Lodge. Photo by Jim Grode.

Distance: 4.4 miles one-way (3.9 miles on MST plus 0.5-mile spur to parking); 8.8 miles round-trip

Degree of difficulty: Moderate to strenuous

Trail type: Natural-surface trail

Trailhead 1: Craven Gap parking area (BRP MP 377.4); no facilities

Trailhead 1 coordinates: N35.64807, W82.49171

Trailhead 1 elevation: 3,156 feet

Trailhead 2: Tanbark Ridge Tunnel parking area (BRP MP 376.7); no facilities

Trailhead 2 coordinates: N35.66563, W82.46186

Trailhead 2 elevation: 3,319 feet

Total elevation change: gain, 1,596 feet; loss, 1,433 feet

MST segment: 3

Highlights: History at Rattlesnake Lodge ruins; wildflowers

Dogs: Allowed on leash

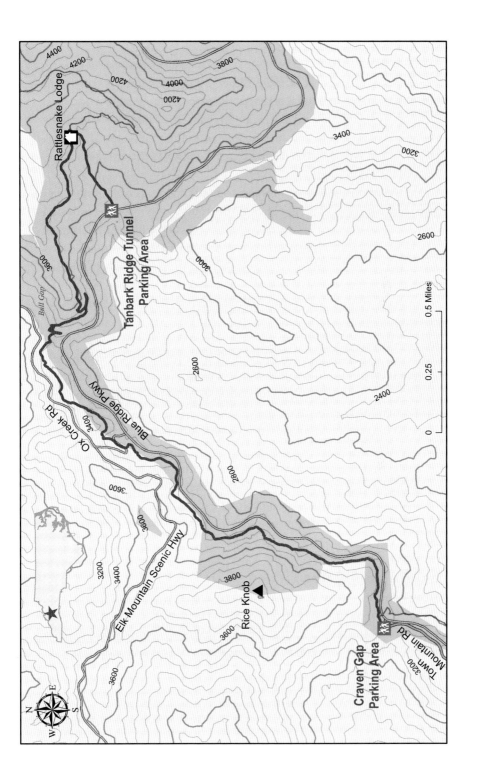

HIKE OVERVIEW

This section of the MST, a mere fifteen-minute drive from downtown Asheville, received national attention in 2010, when President and Mrs. Obama walked it while on a vacation in town. Their good taste in hiking destinations is clear to anyone who follows in their footsteps. The hike is relatively flat, with an easy trail tread, and is known for its spring wildflowers and historical ruins.

From parking at Craven Gap, a short spur trail ascends a set of stairs before reaching the MST proper. The trail contours along through hardwood forests above the BRP for 1.4 miles before crossing Elk Mountain Scenic Highway (which also has a small gravel parking area). It continues over a small knob, then drops into Bull Gap. A short trail here leads to another small parking area on Ox Creek Rd.

Just beyond Bull Gap, the MST begins its only real ascent on this hike, climbing more than 500 feet over the next mile, via a series of switchbacks. Once the trail levels out, it is about another 0.5 mile to the site of Rattlesnake Lodge, a summer home built by Asheville physician and early Carolina Mountain Club leader Chase Ambler in 1903–4. Informational panels provide some history and a diagram of the remaining ruins, and the Carolina Mountain Club's *Trail Profiles and Maps* (see "For More Information" below) provides additional historical information about Ambler and the lodge.

From the lodge site, a right turn onto a spur trail descends to the end of the hike on the BRP at Tanbark Ridge Tunnel. For a slightly longer walk, hikers may continue straight on the MST to a second spur trail 0.2 mile ahead that leads to the same point on the BRP.

DRIVING DIRECTIONS

From Asheville, drive north on the BRP. From the Folk Art Center (MP 382.0), it is about 4.6 miles to Craven Gap (MP 377.4), Trailhead 1, which is on the left at the intersection of the BRP and Town Mountain Rd. Continue another 2.9 miles to Trailhead 2 (MP 374.5), at wide gravel parking areas on both sides of the road just before the Tanbark Ridge Tunnel.

HIKE DIRECTIONS

0.0 From the Craven Gap parking area, head up a set of stairs. After 100 yards, continue straight to join the MST.

0.7 Ascend another short set of stairs.

0.9 Cross a stream, then take the left fork at the Y-intersection.

1.4 At a gravel parking area, continue straight across Elk Mountain Scenic Highway.

1.7 Pass a trail on the left, which leads to a gravel parking area on Ox Creek Rd.

2.4 Continue straight past another trail on the left, which leads to the Bull Gap gravel parking area on Ox Creek Rd.

2.5 Begin ascending a series of switchbacks.

3.9 At the ruins of Rattlesnake Lodge, turn right onto the first spur trail leading to the BRP. If you wish to continue farther, a second trail on the right 0.2 mile ahead also leads to the BRP.

4.4 Complete the hike at a parking area on the BRP at the Tanbark Ridge Tunnel.

SPECIAL CONSIDERATIONS

The BRP is often closed during the winter or in inclement weather, making access to this hike difficult or impossible. If you are unsure whether the parkway is open, check the National Park Service's "Blue Ridge Parkway Road Closure Map" (www.nps.gov/blri/planyourvisit/roadclosures.htm) for real-time closure information.

FOR MORE INFORMATION

BRP: www.nps.gov/blri

BRP Maps: www.nps.gov/blri/planyourvisit/maps.htm

Carolina Mountain Club website (trail maintainers in this segment): www.carolinamountainclub.org

Walt Weber and "the Gang" for the Carolina Mountain Club, *Trail Profiles and Maps: From Clingmans Dome to Mount Mitchell and Beyond* (3rd ed. 2018), has detailed elevation profiles and maps for Segments 1–3 of the MST, as well as historical information about several of the areas covered in this book.

Hike 7
THE CRAGGIES

Glassmine Falls Overlook to Graybeard Overlook

Springtime near Glassmine Falls Overlook. Photo by Jim Grode.

Distance: 2.3 miles one-way; 4.6 miles round-trip
Degree of difficulty: Moderate
Trail type: Natural-surface trail
Trailhead 1: Glassmine Falls Overlook (BRP MP 361.2); no facilities
Trailhead 1 coordinates: N35.73423, W82.34419
Trailhead 1 elevation: 5,186 feet
Trailhead 2: Graybeard Overlook (BRP MP 363.4); no facilities
Trailhead 2 coordinates: N35.71096, W82.36410
Trailhead 2 elevation: 5,600 feet
Total elevation change: gain, 1,046 feet; loss, 632 feet
MST segment: 3
Highlights: Views; wildflowers; berries
Dogs: Allowed on leash

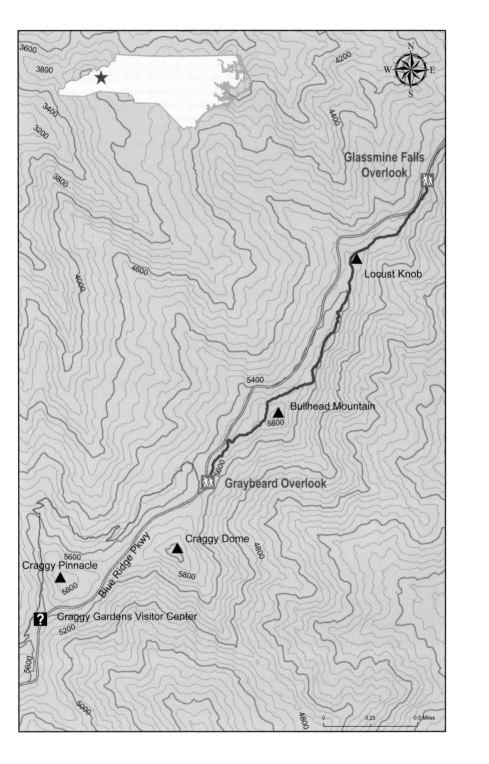

Glassmine Falls Overlook 🚶🚶

▲ Locust Knob

5400

▲ Bullhead Mountain
5800

🚶🚶 **Graybeard Overlook**
5600

▲ Craggy Dome
5800

Craggy Pinnacle
5600
▲ 5800

Blue Ridge Pkwy

❓ **Craggy Gardens Visitor Center**
5200

N
W · E
S

3600
3800
4200
3800
3400
3200
4400
3800
4600
4000
4600
4800
5600
5000
4800

0   0.25   0.5 Miles

HIKE OVERVIEW

This hike combines gnarly high-altitude spruce-fir and birch forest, heath balds, striking views, and, in season, plentiful wildflowers, blueberries, and blackberries. (Feel free to gorge yourself on the berries, but please leave the flowers for others to enjoy.) Its close proximity to Asheville and short distance make it a good choice for a quick afternoon stroll.

The hike begins at the back of Glassmine Falls Overlook, where a marked trail enters the woods. It continues over a small knob, then reaches the BRP and continues along the shoulder for about 100 yards before returning to the woods. Beginning at mile 1.0, it crosses over a couple of rock outcroppings, then through a meadow with seasonal wildflowers.

At mile 1.4, the trail reaches "Lunch Rock." A short walk around to the back of the rock, then an easy scramble up, leads to an excellent spot for a break, with 360-degree views over the nearby heath and the surrounding mountains.

Continuing through alternating heath balds and spruce-fir forests, the trail passes near the summit of Bullhead Mountain (5,899 feet) and then a wind shelter made of rhododendron branches on the left. On the subsequent descent, note a spectacular gnarled birch at mile 2.2 before reaching Graybeard Overlook and the end of the hike.

DRIVING DIRECTIONS

From Asheville, drive north on the BRP. From the Folk Art Center (MP 382.0), it is about 19 miles to Graybeard Overlook (MP 363.4), Trailhead 2, on the right. From here, it is another 2.2 miles to Trailhead 1, Glassmine Falls Overlook (MP 361.2), again on the right.

HIKE DIRECTIONS

0.0 Begin the hike at the back of Glassmine Falls Overlook, entering the woods on the marked trail.

0.2 Cross over a small knob, then reach the BRP and walk along the shoulder outside the guardrail.

0.3 Return to the woods on the trail.

1.0 Cross over a rock outcrop.

1.1 Cross another rock outcrop.

1.2 Pass through a meadow.

1.4 Pass Lunch Rock on the left, with 360-degree views over the heath bald. Walk around on the side trail to climb up the back side of the rock.

1.5 Pass a rock outcrop on the left.

1.8 Pass near the summit of Bullhead Mountain and begin descending.

1.9 In an open forest, pass a wind shelter made of rhododendron branches on the left.

2.2 Pass a big gnarled birch.

2.3 Reach Graybeard Overlook and the end of the hike.

SPECIAL CONSIDERATIONS

The BRP is often closed during the winter or in inclement weather, making access to this hike difficult or impossible. If you are unsure whether the parkway is open, check the National Park Service's "Blue Ridge Parkway Road Closure Map" (www.nps.gov/blri/planyourvisit/roadclosures.htm) for real-time closure information.

FOR MORE INFORMATION

BRP: www.nps.gov/blri

BRP Maps: www.nps.gov/blri/planyourvisit/maps.htm

Carolina Mountain Club website (trail maintainers in this segment): www.carolinamountainclub.org

Walt Weber and "the Gang" for the Carolina Mountain Club, *Trail Profiles and Maps: From Clingmans Dome to Mount Mitchell and Beyond* (3rd ed. 2018), has detailed elevation profiles and maps for Segments 1–3 of the MST, as well as historical information about several of the areas covered in this book.

Hike 8

LINVILLE GORGE *Wolf Pit Road to Table Rock*

The MST near Shortoff Mountain. Photo by Christine White.

Distance: 8.4 miles one-way (6.8 miles on MST plus 1.0-mile spur from parking at Wolf Pit Rd. and 0.6-mile out-and-back spur to Table Rock summit); 16.8 miles round-trip

Degree of difficulty: Strenuous

Trail type: Natural-surface trail

Trailhead 1: End of Wolf Pit Rd.; no facilities

Trailhead 1 coordinates: N35.82414, W81.88957

Trailhead 1 elevation: 1,777 feet

Trailhead 2: Table Rock parking lot; picnic, restrooms

Trailhead 2 coordinates: N35.88646, W81.88474

Trailhead 2 elevation: 3,386 feet

Total elevation change: gain, 3,573 feet; loss, 1,964 feet

MST segment: 4

Highlights: Maybe the best views of Linville Gorge; the most challenging hike in this book

Dogs: Allowed on leash

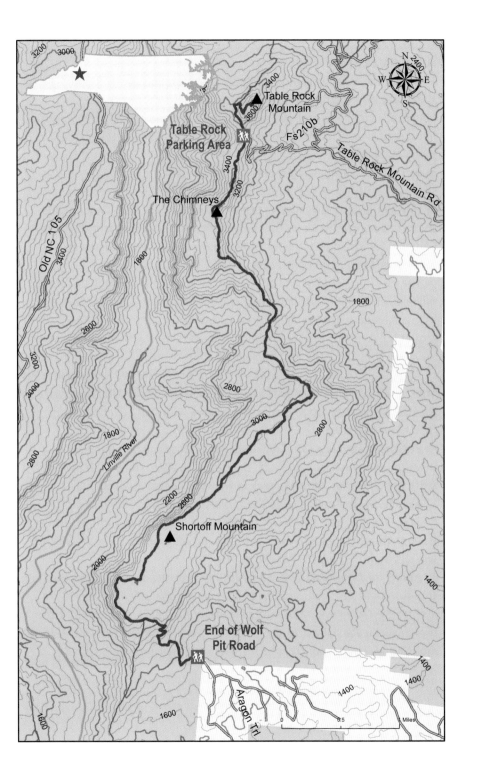

3200 3000

N 2400
W ● E
S

Table Rock
Mountain

3600

Table Rock
Parking Area

Fs 210b

3400

The Chimneys

Table Rock Mountain Rd

3200

Old NC 105

3400

1600

1800

2600

3200

2800

2000

1800

3000

2800

1800

Linville River

2800

3000

2200

2600

Shortoff Mountain

2000

1400

End of Wolf
Pit Road

1400

1600

1400

1400

Aragon Trl

1600

0   0.5   Miles

HIKE OVERVIEW

This hike, the most challenging one in this book, features an impressive 3,500 feet of climbing over more than 8 miles, few water sources, and a long shuttle for hikers not wishing to make it a round-trip hike. Moreover, because this area has had frequent forest fires, there is little shade for much of the hike.

As great as the challenges may be, the rewards are equally great. This section of trail includes perhaps the best views into the 2,000-foot depths of Linville Gorge, often called the Grand Canyon of the East. Other points command impressive views over Lake James and the Piedmont of North Carolina. For naturalists, the forest fires have created many opportunities to see forest regeneration in action.

The hike begins at the end of Wolf Pit Rd. with a steady climb up a 1.0-mile spur trail, then continues straight onto the MST. After another 0.3 mile of climbing, the trail levels out just below the summit of Shortoff Mountain, continuing along the rim of Linville Gorge without significant elevation change for the next 2.4 miles.

At mile 2.0, an unusual pond sits on top of the mountain. However, it is often dry, so you can't rely on it as a water source. Shortly after the pond, the trail passes through a heavily burned area with little vegetation other than mountain laurel.

Beginning at mile 3.7, the trail descends, with a few short uphills, for 1.3 miles to Chimney Gap. From here, the trail once again steadily ascends to reach the Chimneys, dramatic rock formations on the rim of the canyon.

At mile 7.0, the trail reaches the Table Rock parking lot, which is Trailhead 2, but the hike continues another 0.7 mile to the summit. Walk through the parking lot to the north side and continue on the MST, which will join up with the Table Rock Trail.

At the junction with the Little Table Rock Trail, the MST and Table Rock Trail turn right. Less than 100 yards later, at the split, the hike leaves the MST for the Table Rock Trail. This trail leads to the Table Rock summit, with more spectacular views, in 0.3 mile. After exploring the summit, turn around and retrace your steps to the parking lot to complete the hike.

DRIVING DIRECTIONS

Leaving from Morganton, to reach Trailhead 1, the end of Wolf Pit Rd., head west on Green St. (NC 181). About 0.5 mile after crossing the Catawba River, turn left at the traffic light onto West NC 126. In 0.6 mile, at a traffic light just before Freedom High School, turn right to stay on NC 126. Continue on NC 126 11.2 miles. At 10.6 miles, the road reaches the shore of Lake James at a long right-hand curve, then passes a boat ramp. This is the signal that you are near your next turn. Approximately 0.2 mile after leaving the lake-shore, turn right on gravel Wolf Pit Rd. Continue on this road 2.5 miles to the trailhead.

To reach Trailhead 2 from Trailhead 1, return to NC 126 and turn left. After 1.3 miles, turn left on Fish Hatchery Rd. (Coming from Morganton, turn right on Fish Hatchery Rd. 9.9 miles after turning in front of Freedom High.) Travel 2.8 miles on this road to a left turn onto Forest Service Rd. 210. This turn, onto the first of two gravel roads next to each other, may be easy to miss; it is approximately 0.4 mile past the intersection with Faulkner Hill Rd. Continue 11.5 miles to a Y-intersection. Take the left fork and continue 1.4 miles to the parking area.

HIKE DIRECTIONS

0.0 From the end of Wolf Pit Rd., walk past a kiosk onto the trail to begin this hike. The trail climbs steadily for the next 1.3 miles.

0.2 At a three-way intersection with a directional sign for Shortoff Mountain, turn right. Continue up a section with log steps.

0.6 Turn right (uphill) at a switchback where a primitive trail continues straight.

0.7 At an overlook of Lake James, make a switchback to the left.

0.8 Switchback right, then left at another overlook.

1.0 At a signed junction, continue straight on the MST.

1.3 Reach a level plateau and follow the lip of Linville Gorge. The trail will not descend or ascend significantly for another 2.4 miles.

1.4 Follow a narrow passage across a crevice and past a seep that is a possible, but not abundant, water source.

1.8 Continue past a trail on the right and continue left (north) along the ridge.

2.0 Pass an unusual pond, often dry, on top of the mountain.

2.2 Pass through a desolate burned-over area with lots of downed wood and charred trunks where mountain laurel is the only live vegetation of any size.

3.7 Begin descending.

4.4 Reach the top of small knob.

4.6 Pass a fire ring on the ridge; the trees here have not been burned.

4.7 Turn sharply right to descend to Chimney Gap. (It's easy to miss this turn.) The Cambric Trail (Forest Service Trail (FST) 234), which is not maintained, follows the ridge into the gorge.

5.0 Reach a saddle with campsites and begin climbing again.

6.3 Turn right (north), following the west side of the ridge with views of the gorge and river, looking along the gorge side of the Chimneys and to Table Rock ahead.

6.6 Follow the west side of the ridge into the Chimneys, passing around and among remarkable shapes and stacks of rock.

6.7 Continue on the top of the ridge past the Chimneys.

7.0 Reach the Table Rock parking lot and continue on the MST from the north side of the parking lot, joining the Table Rock Trail.

7.4 At the junction with the Little Table Rock Trail (FST 236), turn right to stay on the MST and Table Rock Trail. In less than 100 yards, the MST and Table Rock Trail separate; continue ascending right on the Table Rock Trail.

7.7 Reach the Table Rock summit and retrace your steps to the parking lot.

8.4 Reach the Table Rock parking lot again—the end of the hike.

SPECIAL CONSIDERATIONS

Both trailheads are at the ends of dirt roads that may be difficult or impassible for low-clearance cars or after wet weather.

Parking at either trailhead can be scarce on weekends, so plan to arrive early.

The Table Rock picnic area closes to motor vehicles seasonally, usually from January through early April. To complete this hike during the closures, it may be necessary to park farther down and walk a portion of the road.

FOR MORE INFORMATION

Linville Gorge and Mount Mitchell (National Geographic Map #779): www.natgeomaps.com/linville-gorge-mount-mitchell-pisgah -national-forest

Linville Gorge Wilderness Map (US Forest Service): theforeststore.com /product/linville-gorge-wildnerness-map (note the misspelling "wildnerness" is in the URL itself)

Grandfather Ranger District: www.fs.usda.gov/recarea/nfsnc/recreation /hiking/recarea/?recid=48954&actid=51

Hike 9

WATERFALLS *Pineola Road to Roseboro Road*

Gragg Prong Falls.
Photo by Robert Trawick.

Distance: 3.6 miles one-way; 7.2 miles round-trip
Degree of difficulty: Moderate but requires some wading
Trail type: Natural-surface trail
Trailhead 1: Pineola Rd. parking lot; no facilities
Trailhead 1 coordinates: N36.00750, W81.80104
Trailhead 1 elevation: 2,410 feet
Trailhead 2: Roseboro Rd. parking area; no facilities
Trailhead 2 coordinates: N36.03197, W81.80363
Trailhead 2 elevation: 2,130 feet
Total elevation change: gain, 811 feet; loss, 1,090 feet
MST segment: 4
Highlights: Hunt Fish Falls, Gragg Prong Falls, numerous smaller falls and swimming holes; easiest, shortest, most accessible stretch in this part of the MST
Dogs: Allowed on leash

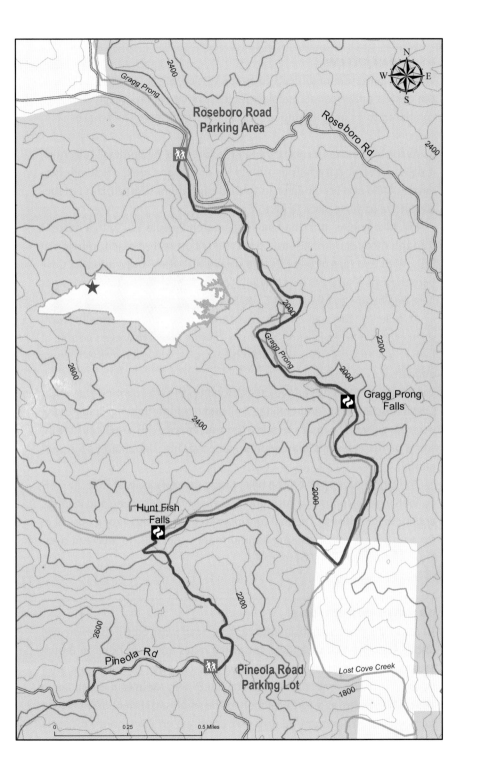

Roseboro Road
Parking Area

Gragg Prong

2400

Roseboro Rd

2400

2000

Gragg Prong

2200

2000

Gragg Prong
Falls

2600

2400

2000

Hunt Fish
Falls

2600

2200

Pineola Rd

Pineola Road
Parking Lot

Lost Cove Creek

1800

0   0.25   0.5 Miles

HIKE OVERVIEW

Within a remote and difficult-to-reach section of the MST, this is one of the easiest and most accessible stretches. What it may lack in challenge compared to its neighboring sections, however, it more than makes up in scenery.

As the hike makes its way through the Lost Cove Wilderness Study Area, it passes several waterfalls on tributaries of Wilson Creek, a federally designated Wild and Scenic River. As these designations suggest, this is a special and rewarding place to hike.

The hike begins at a small parking area on Pineola Rd., with a descent through rhododendron to Lost Cove Creek. At 0.7 mile, it reaches Hunt Fish Falls, with two falls of 6 to 8 feet; a smaller tributary drops into Lost Cove here through a series of falls totaling 50 feet in height. The trail turns right here and begins to follow Lost Cove Creek downstream.

At mile 1.3, the trail crosses Lost Cove Creek. Under normal circumstances, this is an easy wade, and more nimble hikers may even be able to rock-hop without getting wet; after heavy rains, however, it may become difficult or even impassible.

Shortly after the Lost Cove Creek crossing, the trail continues straight past a junction with Timber Ridge Trail and begins following Gragg Prong upstream. Over the next 1.6 miles, the trail crosses this creek four times; some of the crossings may require some wading, depending on recent rainfall.

The largest waterfall on the hike, Gragg Prong Falls, is at mile 2.2. This 35-foot-high fall ends in a large pool, excellent for swimming and wading, and rocks for sunning. The trail continues to follow Gragg Prong upstream for another 1.4 miles, passing several more waterfalls, rapids, and overlooks, before reaching Roseboro Rd.

DRIVING DIRECTIONS

To reach the trailheads from Morganton, head west on NC 181. From the bridge over the Catawba River, travel 11.3 miles and turn right on Brown Mountain Beach Rd. at Smyrna Baptist Church. After 5.1 miles, just after crossing Wilson Creek, turn left to stay on Brown Mountain Beach Rd. In another 8.7 miles, at a T-intersection in the small settlement of Mortimer, turn left onto Edgemont Rd. (NC 90). Continue on Edgemont Rd. for 1.8

miles to the intersection with Pineola Rd., where the routes to the two trailheads diverge.

To reach Trailhead 1, turn left on Pineola Rd. and continue 3.0 miles to the trailhead on the right.

To reach Trailhead 2, continue straight on Edgemont Rd. for another 0.2 mile to a four-way intersection just past a bridge. Turn left and continue 4.2 miles to the trailhead, on the left just past a bridge over Gragg Prong.

To reach the trailheads from Linville or Blowing Rock, head south on Linville Ave. (US 221 Business) from the intersection of US 221 and NC 105. After 0.3 mile, at an all-way stop, turn left on Roseboro Rd. Continue 5.7 miles on Roseboro Rd. (crossing the BRP after 1.7 miles) to reach Trailhead 2. To reach Trailhead 1 from here, continue 4.2 miles to a four-way intersection and turn right on Edgemont Rd. After 0.2 mile, turn right on Pineola Rd. Trailhead 1 is 3.0 miles ahead on the right.

HIKE DIRECTIONS

0.0 From the parking area on Pineola Rd., head north on the trail marked with a sign for "Hunt Fish Falls," indicating that the trail is also FST 263.

0.4 Begin following a small creek.

0.7 Reach Lost Cove Creek at a trail junction near the top of Hunt Fish Falls. Turn right, following the creek downstream.

1.3 Wade across the creek and go right.

1.4 Continue straight through a junction with the Timber Ridge Trail (FST 261), then begin climbing a bank up the west side of Gragg Prong.

1.6 Cross Gragg Prong; this crossing usually requires wading.

2.2 Descend toward 35-foot Gragg Prong Falls, with good swimming, wading, and sunning.

2.5 Cross Gragg Prong.

2.6 Cross Gragg Prong again, rock-hopping.

2.7 Pass by a side trail to an overlook a few yards from the trail.

3.1 Pass another nice side trail to rocks and rapids, where there are a 3-foot waterfall and several pools.

3.2 Wade across Gragg Prong one more time.

3.6 Reach the end of the hike at the parking area on Roseboro Rd.

SPECIAL CONSIDERATIONS

Reaching the trailheads requires driving on gravel roads. Under most conditions, they are passable by all cars, but after severe weather, they may become difficult or impossible for low-clearance cars.

The trailheads can become congested, especially on summer weekends, so try to get an early start.

FOR MORE INFORMATION

Linville Gorge and Mount Mitchell (National Geographic Map #779): www.natgeomaps.com/linville-gorge-mount-mitchell-pisgah -national-forest

Wilson Creek / Harper Creek / Lost Cove Areas: Wilson Creek Visitor Center, 7805 Brown Mountain Beach Rd., Collettsville, 28611, 828-759- 0005; map available at www.nationalforestmapstore.com/product-p /nc-16.htm

Wilson Creek Visitor Center: www.explorecaldwell.com/wilson-creek -visitor-center

Grandfather Ranger District: www.fs.usda.gov/recarea/nfsnc/recreation /hiking/recarea/?recid=48954&actid=51

Hike 10

CONE MANOR CARRIAGE TRAILS

Shulls Mill Road to Flat Top Manor

Flat Top Manor. Photo by Glenn Strouhal.

Distance: 4.3 miles one-way; 8.6 miles round-trip
Degree of difficulty: Moderate
Trail type: Natural-surface trail
Trailhead 1: Shulls Mill Rd. parking lot; no facilities
Trailhead 1 coordinates: N36.15965, W81.71787
Trailhead 1 elevation: 3,687 feet
Trailhead 2: Flat Top Manor parking lot (BRP MP 294.0); water, restrooms
Trailhead 2 coordinates: N36.14888, W81.69273
Trailhead 2 elevation: 3,972 feet
Total elevation change: gain, 1,002 feet; loss, 717 feet
MST segment: 5
Highlights: Scenery; history and crafts at Flat Top Manor
Dogs: Allowed on leash

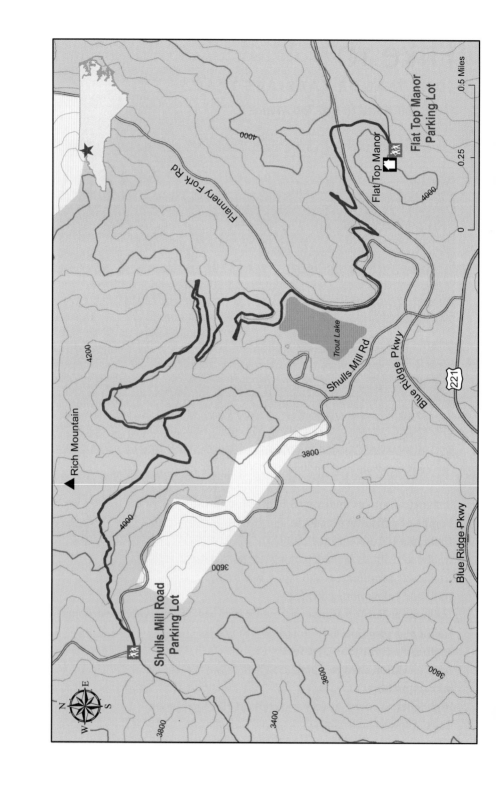

HIKE OVERVIEW

This hike is primarily in the BRP's Moses H. Cone Memorial Park, the former summer estate of Gilded Age textile entrepreneur, conservationist, and philanthropist Moses Cone. A nature lover, Cone carefully developed 25 miles of carriage roads on his estate to allow him to enjoy the land to its greatest extent. These roads have been maintained as wide, gentle trails for hikers, skiers, and equestrians. The MST takes advantage of the park's trail system, following these old carriage roads for most of this hike. Flat Top Manor, Cone's luxurious home at the end of the hike, now hosts the Parkway Craft Center, which exhibits and sells works by artisans from throughout the Appalachian region. It is open 10:00 A.M.–5:00 P.M. daily from April through November.

The hike begins at a small parking lot on Shulls Mill Rd. Turning right (toward Blowing Rock), it travels about 75 yards on the road shoulder to reach a set of stairs on the left that lead to the trail. After half a mile, the trail passes over a stile, which marks the boundary of Moses H. Cone Memorial Park, then turns right on a gravel road. (The left turn leads to a spiral trail up Rich Mountain.)

The trail soon enters a large pasture, where the route makes a right turn, then a left. After continuing on the gentle trail through the woods for 1.7 miles, the trail forks. The MST continues on the left fork, and the right fork leads to the Trout Lake parking, which is an option if you were unable to find a space at Flat Top Manor or want a shorter hike.

The hike continues across the dam that forms Trout Lake and along the lakeshore before entering another pasture. Here the trail goes under the BRP, finally reaching Flat Top Manor. Restrooms and water are available here, as well as the items for sale in the craft center.

DRIVING DIRECTIONS

From the intersection of the BRP and US 321 near Blowing Rock, drive south on the BRP. After 2.3 miles, turn left on the entrance road for Cone Manor House at MP 294.1. Trailhead 2 is here.

To drive to Trailhead 1, return to the BRP, turn left, and drive south 0.5 mile to a left turn signed to US 221. Before reaching US 221, turn right on Shulls Mill Rd., then pass back under the BRP. Just past the BRP, bear left to stay on Shulls Mill Rd. Continue 1.7 miles to the parking for Trailhead 1, a gravel pullout on the left where Shulls Mill Rd. makes a 90-degree right turn.

Flat Top Manor is very popular, and the lot may fill up early. Alternate parking near Trailhead 2 is available at Trout Lake, mile 2.9 of the hike. To reach this parking, follow the directions toward Trailhead 1. The entrance to the parking area is on the right 0.4 mile after Shulls Mill Rd. passes under the BRP.

HIKE DIRECTIONS

0.0 From the parking lot, turn right (toward Blowing Rock) on Shulls Mill Rd. and walk 75 yards on the shoulder. Turn left to take wooden steps up the hillside, into the woods. The trail climbs 500 feet in elevation in the next 0.5 mile.

0.5 Climb over a step stile to reach a gravel road, which is part of Moses H. Cone Memorial Park's carriage trail system. Turn right onto that road, known as the Rich Mountain Trail.

1.1 At a T-intersection in a pasture, turn right.

1.2 Just before reentering the woods, turn left onto a trail leading to Trout Lake.

1.5 In the next 0.3 mile, cross over three culverted streams before reaching a gate.

2.2 Continue past a short side trail to a stream on the north side near a small dam.

2.9 When the trail forks, go left to continue on the MST. If you parked at Trout Lake, turn right here and cross the bridge, then walk about 0.3 mile to the parking area.

3.1 Cross over the Trout Lake dam and continue to the right on a carriage trail along the lake.

3.3 Take the left fork going to the manor house.

3.5 Cross Flannery Fork Rd. and follow the trail toward the manor house.

4.1 At the T-intersection, go right through a tunnel under the BRP. The trail passes in front of the carriage house.

4.2 Reach Flat Top Manor and the end of the hike. (The MST continues on the unsigned trail to the left shortly before the house.)

SPECIAL CONSIDERATIONS

The BRP is often closed during the winter or in inclement weather, making access to this hike difficult or impossible. If you are unsure whether the parkway is open, check the National Park Service's "Blue Ridge Parkway Road Closure Map" (www.nps.gov/blri/planyourvisit/roadclosures.htm) for real-time closure information.

FOR MORE INFORMATION

BRP: www.nps.gov/blri

BRP Maps: www.nps.gov/blri/planyourvisit/maps.htm

Moses H. Cone Memorial Park carriage trails: www.nps.gov/blri
   /planyourvisit/moses-cone-trails.htm

Hike 11

THE BLUE RIDGE ESCARPMENT

Cascades Recreation Area to Benge Gap

Cascade Falls.
Photo by Barbara Collie.

Distance: 4.1 miles one-way; 8.2 miles round-trip
Degree of difficulty: Moderate
Trail type: Natural-surface trail
Trailhead 1: Cascades Recreation Area (BRP MP 271.9); water, restrooms, picnic tables
Trailhead 1 coordinates: N36.24564, W81.45795
Trailhead 1 elevation: 3,560 feet
Trailhead 2: Benge Gap (BRP MP 268.0); water
Trailhead 2 coordinates: N36.28025, W81.41457
Trailhead 2 elevation: 3,355 feet
Total elevation change: gain, 870 feet; loss, 1,075 feet
MST segment: 5
Highlights: Views; waterfall; woodlands; geologic interest
Dogs: Allowed on leash

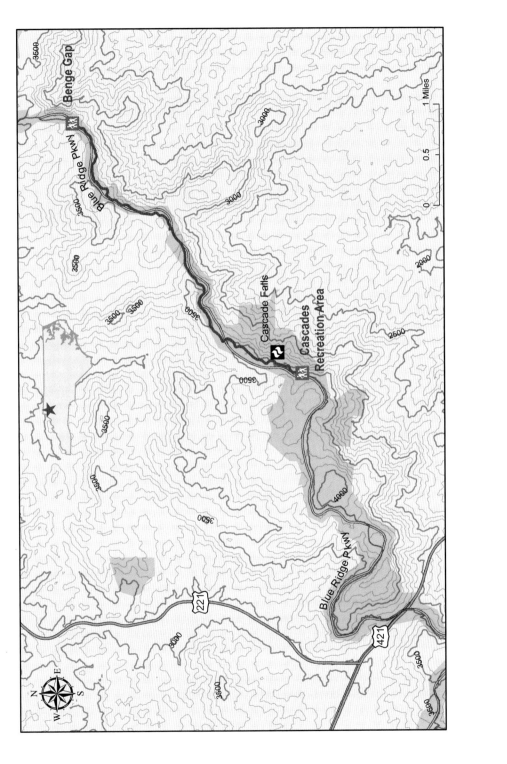

Benge Gap

Blue Ridge PKWY

3500

3500

3500

3500

3500

3500

3500

3500

3500

3500

3600

3600

3600

3600

3600

3000

3000

3000

3000

3000

2000

2600

4000

Cascade Falls

Cascades
Recreation Area

221

Blue Ridge PKWY

421

N
W E
S

0   0.5   1 Miles

HIKE OVERVIEW

Much of the MST between Beacon Heights and Devils Garden Overlook runs along the Blue Ridge escarpment, the dramatic 220-million-year-old geologic upheaval marking the delineation of the Southern Appalachians and the Piedmont. Nowhere on the MST is the escarpment more apparent than on this hike, where the trail rarely leaves the edge of the cliff and it is not unusual for the mountain to lose 1,300 feet of altitude in less than half a mile.

The hike begins at the north end of the Cascades Recreation Area parking lot, which has restrooms (open May–October) and picnic tables. After a few yards, the trail splits; the MST and this hike follow the left-hand fork of this loop trail.

At mile 0.3 the right-hand fork of the loop returns to the MST, which continues to the left and uphill. It is well worth taking a short detour downhill here to see Cascade Falls, a beautiful multilevel falls that drops more than 250 feet in several free falls and slides.

The trail continues across the BRP and gradually rises to travel high above the parkway, then descends to cross a pasture and return to the BRP at Phillips Gap (3,221 feet). It continues on the BRP for 0.3 mile, passing Phillips Gap Rd. While walking along the BRP, be sure to face oncoming traffic because of narrow shoulders and short sight lines.

Where a second section of Phillips Gap Rd. goes off to the right, the MST goes into the woods on the left. It goes uphill briefly before leveling off.

The trail crosses another pasture, keeping near the tree line on the right, then crosses the BRP diagonally to continue across another pasture and into a nice woodland area. The trail continues, never far away from the BRP, for another 1.4 miles before returning to the BRP just before the end of the hike.

DRIVING DIRECTIONS

Both trailheads are on the BRP north of Boone. From the interchange of US 421 and the BRP, it is 4.5 miles to the Cascades Recreation Area, Trailhead 1, at MP 271.9. Trailhead 2, Benge Gap, is another 3.9 miles ahead at the intersection of the BRP intersection and Park Vista Rd. (MP 268.0). The Park Vista Inn, just off the parkway, allows hikers to park in its lot, but requires advance notice; call 336-877-5200 or email innkeeper@parkvistainn.com. Alternatively, limited roadside parking is available on the BRP.

HIKE DIRECTIONS

0.0 From the north end of the Cascades Recreation Area, enter the woods following the signs to Cascade Falls. After a few yards on the trail, take the left fork of this loop trail. The trail goes downhill and follows a stream.

0.3 After crossing a bridge, turn left going uphill to follow the MST. Cascade Falls is straight ahead.

1.0 Cross the BRP and go around the chain across a gravel road. Walk 40 feet and turn right to follow the MST.

2.1 Come out of the woods and walk down across a pasture. Walk north on the west shoulder of BRP past Phillips Gap Rd., which goes west.

2.4 Opposite a section of Phillips Gap Rd. that turns gravel and travels east (right), turn left into the woods.

2.7 Cross a pasture, going downhill. Keep near the tree line on the right, heading toward the BRP.

2.8 Cross the BRP diagonally. Look north for the MST sign at the end of the pasture where the woods begin.

4.1 Return to the BRP just south of the intersection with Park Vista Rd. at Benge Gap, the end of this hike.

SPECIAL CONSIDERATIONS

The BRP is often closed during the winter or in inclement weather, making access to this hike difficult or impossible. If you are unsure whether the parkway is open, check the National Park Service's "Blue Ridge Parkway Road Closure Map" (www.nps.gov/blri/planyourvisit/roadclosures.htm), for real-time closure information.

FOR MORE INFORMATION

BRP: www.nps.gov/blri
BRP Maps: www.nps.gov/blri/planyourvisit/maps.htm
Park Vista Inn: www.parkvistainn.com

Hike 12

THE BLUFF MOUNTAIN TRAIL

Basin Cove Overlook to Doughton Park Visitor Center

Bluff Mountain summit. Photo by Abigail Jones.

Distance: 4.3 miles one-way; 8.6 miles round-trip
Degree of difficulty: Moderate
Trail type: Natural-surface trail
Trailhead 1: Basin Cove Overlook (BRP MP 244.7); no facilities
Trailhead 1 coordinates: N36.39084, W81.19972
Trailhead 1 elevation: 3,280 feet
Trailhead 2: Doughton Park Visitor Center (BRP MP 241.1); water, restrooms, picnic
Trailhead 2 coordinates: N36.43392, W81.17724
Trailhead 2 elevation: 3,681 feet
Total elevation change: gain, 1,301 feet; loss, 899 feet
MST segment: 5
Highlights: Views; pastures; wildflowers
Dogs: Allowed on leash

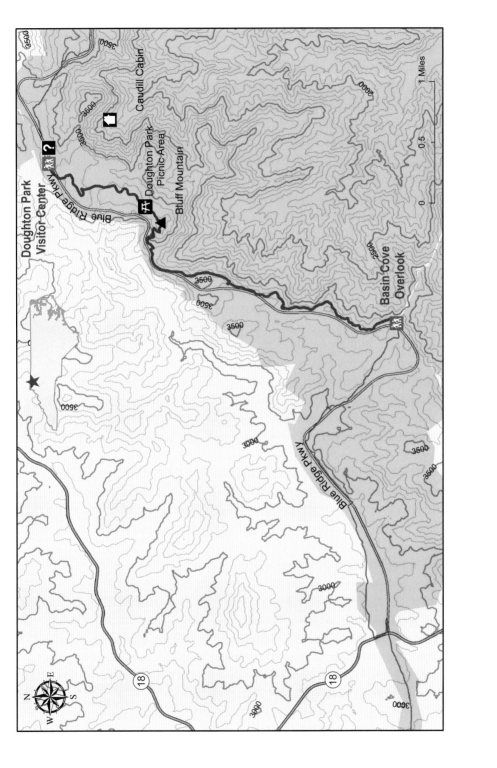

Doughton Park
Visitor Center

Blue Ridge Pkwy

Caudill Cabin

Doughton Park
Picnic Area

Bluff Mountain

Basin Cove
Overlook

Blue Ridge Pkwy

3500

3500

3500

3500

3600

3600

3500

3500

3500

3500

3000

3000

3000

3000

3000

3500

3500

18

18

N
W   E
S

0   0.5   1 Miles

HIKE OVERVIEW

Doughton Park is the BRP's largest recreation area, encompassing 7,000 acres of forests, meadows, and long-range views. Its 30-plus miles of hiking trails offer options for all hikers, from casual to hard-core. The MST, also known as the Bluff Mountain Trail within the park, is an intermediate option that provides a sampling of the different park experiences.

From the Basin Cove Overlook, the hike descends into a hardwood forest. Staying largely parallel to the BRP, the trail skirts the edge of meadows and pastures, but mainly stays in the woods, for the next 1.7 miles before reaching the Bluff Mountain View Overlook (MP 243.4). Although the trail itself stays below the overlook, the view is worth the short climb up a set of stairs.

Returning to the woods, the trail continues to the Alligator Back Overlook. The unusual outcroppings seen from here are geological features composed primarily of schists and gneiss.

From the overlook, the trail climbs about 400 feet in 0.5 mile to reach the top of Bluff Mountain (3,727 feet), with spectacular views. Most of the remaining hike will be through open fields and meadows, with many panoramas, wildflowers, and wildlife-viewing opportunities.

The trail descends to the Doughton Park picnic area, then ascends again to a knob with a picturesque lone tree in a meadow. After passing through a short stretch of woods, it reaches a field with restrooms and a parking area on the left.

The buildings across the field are the old Bluff Mountain Lodge, currently closed. A short spur trail leads from the lodge to the Wildcat Rocks Overlook. To reach it, go through the lodge parking lot to the back right end of the lot. The historic Caudill Cabin is visible 1,500 feet below the overlook.

Beyond the restrooms, the MST goes left, crosses the parking lot driveway, and then crosses the BRP. The end of the hike is across the parking lot at the Bluffs Coffee Shop (also closed) and Doughton Park Visitor Center and Park Store, which sells snacks and drinks (open Thursday through Monday, 10:00 A.M.–5:00 P.M. from late May to early November; closed Tuesdays and Wednesdays). If you have gone out to Wildcat Rock, you may want to remain on the lodge driveway, which rejoins the BRP directly across from the visitor center.

DRIVING DIRECTIONS

Both trailheads are on the Blue Ridge Parkway. Follow the parkway to MP 244.7 for Trailhead 1 or MP 241.1 for Trailhead 2.

HIKE DIRECTIONS

0.0 At the Basin Cove Overlook, look for a break in the wall to find the entrance to the Bluff Mountain Trail and MST on the left. Descend steeply for 300 feet to intersect with the Flat Rock Ridge Trail, which goes right. Go left. Pass a trail sign to stay on the Bluff Mountain Trail and MST on an easy, gradual descent for about 0.5 mile to a footbridge, then an old stile to the right of the trail. Continue to another stile and go through it to join a fire road (part of the Grassy Gap Trail). At this stile, turn left onto the road.

1.0 The MST goes off the Grassy Gap Trail, downhill on the right, about 50 feet before reaching a gate up to the BRP.

1.1 The trail may not be well marked in this part. Soon after you turn into the woods, you'll see a concrete water trough at the bottom of the hill. Do not follow cowpaths leading to that trough; stay straight. The trail stays just below the ridgeline until you come to an open pasture. At the pasture, there are no signs. Turn right and head toward a sign that reads "No horses" where the trail reenters the woods.

1.5 Pass through a turnstile and walk around a bend.

1.7 Reach steps ascending sharply on the left to the Bluff Mountain View Overlook (MP 243.4).

1.9 After crossing a small stream, turn right to ascend a hill.

2.6 Continue through the Alligator Back Overlook parking area (MP 242.3).

3.1 Ascend 400 feet to the top of Bluff Mountain. There are five sets of wooden steps before reaching an outcrop of rocks with spectacular views. Turn left and climb up the rocks to the ridge. Just past the summit, the MST and Bluff Mountain Trail go left toward the BRP. To the right is the Bluff Ridge Primitive Trail. There is a three-sided log-and-stone shelter a few yards down the right trail. The shelter is for viewing, not camping.

3.5 Descend toward the loop road for the Doughton Park picnic area (open seasonally), which you can see from the top of the hill. You are also on the Bluff Mountain Trail, so follow signs for that trail.

3.9 Cross the parking lot, then pass through a stile. Ascend another knob where a lone tree stands in a meadow. Descend into a field and go through another stile; the trail makes a sharp left and begins ascending again.

4.1 Walk past restrooms (open seasonally) on the left. Turn left to stay on the MST, or bear right toward the lodge to take the spur trail to Wildcat Rock.

4.3 Cross the BRP, then reach the end of the hike at the Doughton Park Visitor Center.

SPECIAL CONSIDERATIONS

The BRP is often closed during the winter or in inclement weather, making access to this hike difficult or impossible. If you are unsure whether the parkway is open, check the National Park Service's "Blue Ridge Parkway Road Closure Map" (www.nps.gov/blri/planyourvisit/roadclosures.htm) for real-time closure information.

This section can be extremely hazardous in the winter because the water from the springs ices easily, making the path, even on the wooden steps, treacherous.

FOR MORE INFORMATION

BRP: www.nps.gov/blri
BRP Maps: www.nps.gov/blri/planyourvisit/maps.htm
Doughton Park Trails: www.nps.gov/blri/planyourvisit/doughton-park
-trails.htm

Piedmont Region

Hike 13
STONE MOUNTAIN STATE PARK
Backpack Parking to Upper Trailhead Parking

Cedar Rock from Stone Mountain Trail. Photo by Joe Mickey.

Distance: 5.0 miles one-way (4.7 miles on MST plus 0.3-mile spur);
   10.0 miles round-trip
Degree of difficulty: Strenuous
Trail type: Natural-surface trail
Trailhead 1: Stone Mountain State Park backpack parking lot; no facilities
Trailhead 1 coordinates: N36.39465, W81.06902
Trailhead 1 elevation: 1,362 feet
Trailhead 2: Stone Mountain State Park Upper Trailhead parking lot;
   water, restrooms
Trailhead 2 coordinates: N36.38398, W81.02809
Trailhead 2 elevation: 1,851 feet
Total elevation change: gain, 1,565 feet; loss, 1,076 feet
MST segment: 6
Highlights: History; views; Piedmont forest ecosystem; interesting
   geology
Dogs: Allowed on leash

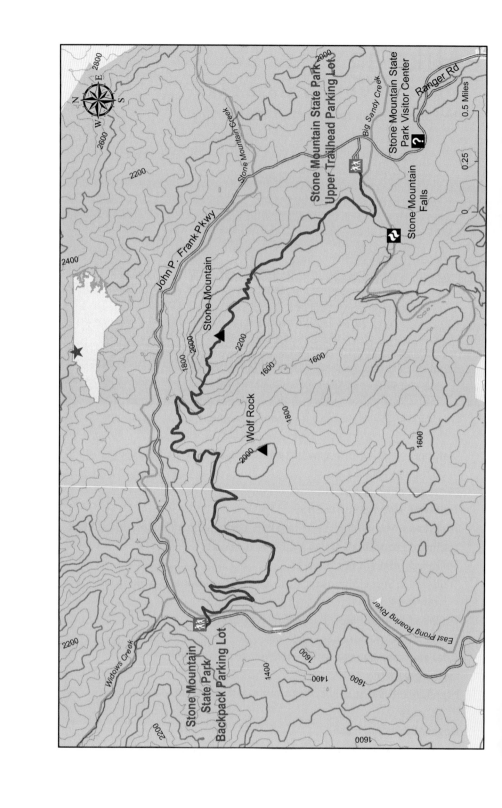

HIKE OVERVIEW

Stone Mountain is a massive granite monolith in the northwestern Piedmont, just below the Blue Ridge Escarpment. The MST makes its descent from the mountain region to the Piedmont here, traveling through Stone Mountain State Park. This hike runs through the heart of the park and over the summit of Stone Mountain. Short optional spurs lead to a reconstructed historic farm and a waterfall. A loop trail provides additional options to lengthen or shorten the hike.

Wilkes County, the home of Stone Mountain State Park, was known as the Moonshine Capital of the World. The area that is now the park was a particular hotbed of moonshining activity because of its remoteness, rugged terrain, and good water. Over 180 stills have been documented in the park, and although this hike does not directly pass by any, a short walk off the trail could easily uncover one.

From the park's Backpack parking lot, the hike begins on the Wolf Rock Trail, which opened in 2019. This trail and another new trail on the east side (not part of this hike) have for the first time brought the MST completely off roads through the park.

After crossing Stone Mountain Rd., the trail crosses the East Prong of Roaring River, a stocked trout fishery. It begins a steady climb on a wide, well-designed trail through hardwood forests, but a few switchbacks keep the grade from becoming too steep. At approximately 1.2 miles, the trail opens up to provide views of Wolf Rock on the right, especially in winter.

After 1.8 miles, the trail reaches a junction, where it joins the old Wolf Rock Trail. The hike continues straight, but the old roadbed to the right leads to Wolf Rock in about 0.3 mile. The trail begins to descend from this junction, occasionally providing views of Stone Mountain.

At mile 2.5, the trail reaches the Stone Mountain Loop Trail. The MST continues to the left, but the trail to the right leads to the historic Hutchinson Homestead, 0.4 mile away. This site, at the base of Stone Mountain with outstanding views of the southern face, was home to four generations of the Hutchinson family beginning in the mid-nineteenth century. It features a log cabin and associated buildings, mostly original to the site, that illustrate the lives of the area's early settlers. The buildings are open on weekends from May through October, but visitors are welcome to walk through the grounds anytime.

At another trail junction at mile 2.6, the MST turns right, following the sign to Stone Mountain. The trail to the left leads less than 0.1 mile to the

Lower Trailhead parking lot, which has restrooms and water. This parking lot allows hikers to shorten the hike by bypassing the Wolf Rock Trail.

After a steady 0.5-mile climb, the trail reaches the rock faces of Stone Mountain. A combination of stairs, boardwalks, and cable guardrails eases the climb and reduces hikers' impact on the mountain's ecosystems. At mile 3.4, the trail crosses the 2,305-foot summit of Stone Mountain, providing spectacular views of the surrounding Blue Ridge Mountains and foothills.

The descent from Stone Mountain, mostly through the woods, is much gentler than the ascent. At mile 4.1, it crosses a small rock face, providing views over the valley to Cedar Rock, on the other side of the hill from Wolf Rock.

After passing a park access road, the MST comes to a junction with the trail to the Upper Trailhead parking lot and picnic area. From the junction, this day hike turns left to leave the MST, continuing on a spur trail to Trailhead 2. Straight ahead on the Stone Mountain Loop and MST, though, a 0.2-mile walk takes you to the top of Stone Mountain Falls, a spectacular 200-foot-tall cascading waterfall with a set of stairs paralleling its length. This short detour is well worth making.

The Stone Mountain Loop Trail continues around the base of the mountain, rejoining the main hike at mile 2.5. The total length of the loop is 4.5 miles, providing several options for lengthening or shortening the hike by starting from and returning to any of the three parking lots.

DRIVING DIRECTIONS

To reach the trailheads from I-77 North, take exit 83 (a left exit) onto US 21 Bypass. Continue on US 21 for 10.7 miles.

To reach the trailheads from I-77 South, take exit 85 for NC 268 Bypass. At the top of the ramp, turn right (west). After 1.0 mile, turn right on US 21 Bypass North, signed to Sparta and Stone Mountain State Park. Continue on US 21 for 9.7 miles.

In either case, turn left on Traphill Rd. The intersection is just past a Dollar General store, where the road widens with a painted median and left-turn lane.

Continue on Traphill Rd. for 4.4 miles, then turn right on John P. Frank Parkway, signed to Stone Mountain State Park. The entrance gate to Stone Mountain State Park is 2.6 miles ahead. Continue another 0.7 mile, passing the park visitor center, to reach Trailhead 2, the Upper Trailhead parking lot, on the left. Trailhead 1, the Backpack parking lot, is on the right 3.2 miles farther along the same road.

HIKE DIRECTIONS

0.0 To begin the hike, take the trail leaving the back left corner of the Backpack parking lot (as seen from the road).

0.1 Cross the paved road and a bridge over the East Prong of Roaring River, then continue onto the gravel road.

0.2 Turn right onto the trail and cross a small bridge.

1.8 Continue straight at a trail sign where an old roadbed goes right. The trail begins to descend.

2.5 At a T-intersection, turn left on the Stone Mountain Loop Trail.

2.6 Cross a footbridge, then go up a set of steps and turn right at the T-intersection, following the sign to Stone Mountain.

2.7 Cross a gravel road leading to the Hutchinson Homestead.

3.2 Continue onto a rock face with a cable guardrail. Over the next 0.1 mile, the trail crosses the rock face several times, with multiple boardwalks, steps, and cables.

3.3 Pass a bench on the left.

3.4 Cross the summit of Stone Mountain.

3.7 Begin descending a set of seven switchbacks.

4.1 Cross a rock face with views of Cedar Rock.

4.6 Pass an access road on the left.

4.7 At a standing chimney, turn left on the trail to the Upper Trailhead parking lot and picnic area. (Another option: continue straight 0.2 mile to reach the top of Stone Mountain Falls.)

5.0 At an open field, take the left fork in the path. Continue to the Upper Trailhead parking lot and the end of the hike.

SPECIAL CONSIDERATIONS

The Upper Trailhead parking lot can become quite crowded on summer weekends. An early start is recommended.

FOR MORE INFORMATION

Stone Mountain State Park Map: files.nc.gov/ncparks/maps-and -brochures/stone-mountain-park-map.pdf

Stone Mountain State Park: www.ncparks.gov/stone-mountain-state
-park
Elkin Valley Trails Association (trail maintainers in this section):
elkinvalleytrails.org

Hike 14

ELKIN AND THE E&A RAIL-TRAIL

Downtown Elkin to US 21 at Collins Road

Elkin directional pole.
Photo by Carolyn Mejia.

Distance: 3.3 miles one-way; 6.6 miles round-trip
Degree of difficulty: Easy
Trail type: Paved road, gravel road, greenway, and natural-surface trail
Trailhead 1: Downtown Elkin; numerous shops with a variety of goods
Trailhead 1 coordinates: N36.24495, W80.84818
Trailhead 1 elevation: 902 feet
Trailhead 2: Intersection of US 21 and Collins Rd.; numerous shops with a variety of goods
Trailhead 2 coordinates: N36.27121, W80.85344
Trailhead 2 elevation: 1,138 feet
Total elevation change: gain, 404 feet; loss, 169 feet
MST segment: 6
Highlights: Small-town downtown; history; scenery; rails-to-trails greenway
Dogs: Allowed on leash

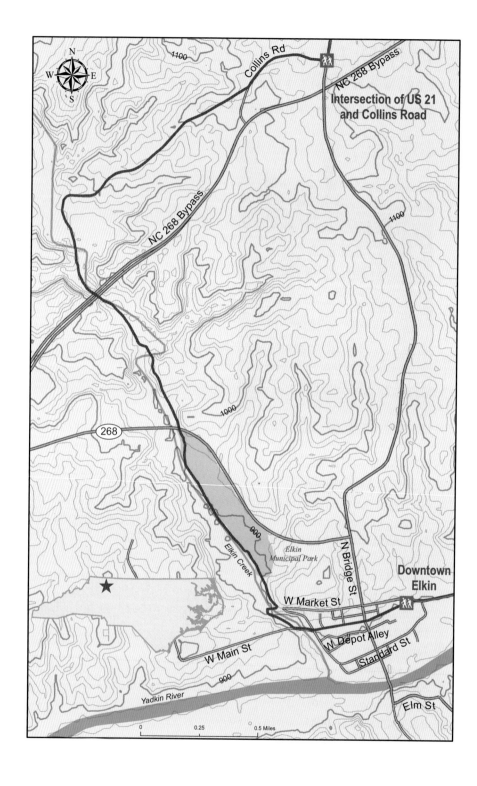

N
W E
S

1100

Collins Rd

NC 268 Bypass

Intersection of US 21
and Collins Road

NC 268 Bypass

1100

1000

268

900

Elkin Creek

Elkin
Municipal Park

N Bridge St

Downtown
Elkin

★

W Market St

W Depot Alley

Standard St

W Main St

900

Yadkin River

Elm St

0   0.25   0.5 Miles

HIKE OVERVIEW

The small town of Elkin, North Carolina, once a textile powerhouse that fell on hard times, has reemerged to embrace a diverse future as, among other things, a trail town and the center of one of North Carolina's largest and best-known winemaking regions. This hike celebrates both the past and future of the town.

The hike begins on the east end of historic downtown Elkin, at an ornamental directional pole that symbolizes Elkin's commitment to trails. The route continues on downtown sidewalks along E. and W. Main St. for 0.3 mile before passing the Elkin library and crossing a bridge over Elkin Creek.

It then turns off the road onto a crushed gravel trail through a small park, past Elkin's Peace Pole and "peace benches" and the 1910 library dam. The trail rejoins the road to cross the creek again and then returns to crushed gravel trail to enter Elkin Municipal Park, which has a variety of recreational facilities.

In the park, the trail passes the Elkin Recreation Center; water and restrooms are available here, as is parking for hikers who want to shorten the walk. Just beyond the recreation center, the trail passes a sculpture, *100 Strong*, commemorating the railroad history of the area and continues onto the old bed of the Elkin & Alleghany Railroad.

Along the E&A Rail-Trail, as this part of the trail is known, are several kiosks with information about the textile and other history of Elkin. The trail also passes a cluster of amenities centered on the old Shoe Factory Dam, which provided water power to several industrial facilities formerly located on Elkin Creek. The trail then crosses a long footbridge over the creek.

Beyond the first footbridge, the trail passes a gong—tradition says first-timers should ring it three times for luck—then crosses a second, 178-foot-long footbridge to reach the Elkin Reservoir. The trail curves to the right around the base of the dam, then joins a gravel access road.

The trail to Collins Rd., which is paved, then continues another 0.4 mile to N. Bridge St. (US 21) and the end of the hike.

DRIVING DIRECTIONS

To reach the trailheads from I-77 North, take exit 83 (a left exit) onto US 21 Bypass. Travel 1.0 mile to the first exit, for NC 268 Bypass. At the top of the ramp, turn left (west).

To reach the trailheads from I-77 South, take exit 85 for NC 268 Bypass. At the top of the ramp, turn right (west), then travel 1.0 mile to the US 21 Bypass interchange.

Coming from either direction, continue west on NC 268 Bypass from the NC 268/US 21 intersection for 0.9 mile to the intersection with N. Bridge St.

To reach Trailhead 2, turn right on N. Bridge St. The intersection with Collins Rd. is at the next traffic light. Parking is available at the large shopping center on the right.

To reach Trailhead 1, turn left from NC 268 Bypass onto N. Bridge St. Travel 2.0 miles to the intersection with Main St. and turn left. The official beginning of the hike is at the ornamental directional pole on the left approximately 0.2 mile ahead; parking is available anywhere on Main St. and in the Liberty parking lot on the right across from the pole.

HIKE DIRECTIONS

0.0 From the ornamental directional pole, head west (left if facing the pole from the road) on E. Main St., past restaurants, shops, and a post office.

0.2 Continue straight across Bridge St. onto W. Main St.

0.3 Cross Front St., then pass the library on the right.

0.4 Cross a bridge over Elkin Creek, then turn right onto a crushed gravel trail into Elkin Peace Park. Pass a peace pole on the left, then an information kiosk on the right.

0.5 Cross Elk Spur St., then turn right to cross the bridge over Elkin Creek on the sidewalk. Turn left onto a crushed gravel path along the left side of N. Front St.

0.6 At a small parking area, follow a path running along Elkin Creek into Elkin Municipal Park, then pass a fishing platform on the left.

0.8 Pass a bridge on the left that crosses Elkin Creek. Cross a culvert over a small stream, then, at a Y-intersection just before some baseball fields, take the left-hand path.

1.1 Continue straight past the Elkin Recreation Center and parking on the right. Pass the *100 Strong* railway sculpture on the right, then continue onto the old bed of the Elkin & Alleghany Railroad.

1.3 Continue under the NC 268 bridge.

1.5 Pass the Shoe Factory Dam, a rain shelter, a bench, a side trail, and a picnic area on the right.

1.6 Cross a large footbridge over Elkin Creek.

1.7 Pass an access road on the left.

1.8 Continue under the dual bridges of NC 286 Bypass.

2.0 Pass another access road on the left and a spur trail on the right.

2.1 Pass a gong on the right, then cross another long bridge over Elkin Creek. Follow the crushed granite path past the reservoir on the right and continue onto the gravel road.

2.9 At the T-intersection, turn left on Collins Rd.

3.3 Reach N. Bridge St. (US 21) and the end of the hike.

FOR MORE INFORMATION

Elkin Valley Trails Association (trail maintainers in this section): elkinvalleytrails.org

What's Up in Elkin: www.whatsupinelkinnc.com

Town of Elkin: www.elkinnc.org

Downtown Elkin: downtownelkin.com

Yadkin Valley / Surry County Tourism: yadkinvalleync.com

There are more than forty-seven vineyards within 30 miles of Elkin in the Yadkin Valley Appellation: www.yadkinvalleywinecountry.com

www.yadkinwinetours.com

www.surrywineries.com/Surry_Wineries/Welcome.html

Hike 15
PILOT MOUNTAIN LOOP

The MST in Pilot Mountain State Park. Photo by Joe Mickey.

Distance: 6.3-mile loop (5.3 on MST, 1.0 on other trail)
Degree of difficulty: Moderate
Trail type: Natural-surface trail
Trailhead elevation: Pinnacle Hotel Rd. parking lot; restrooms
Trailhead elevation: N36.32853, W80.46321
Trailhead elevation: 1,061 feet
Total elevation change: gain, 1,137 feet; loss, 1,137 feet
MST segment: 7
Highlights: Iconic peak; mature forest
Dogs: Allowed on leash

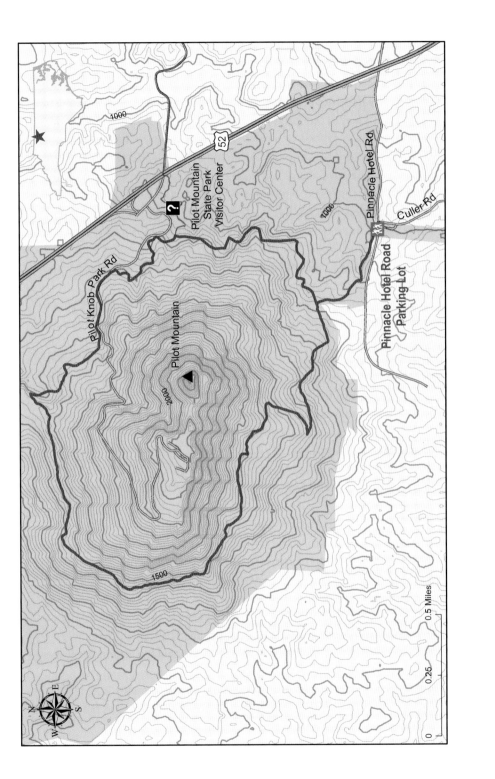

HIKE OVERVIEW

This hike circumnavigates the base of Pilot Mountain, a quartzite monadnock, or isolated mountain, rising above the surrounding Piedmont to 2,421 feet. Known to the Saura people as Jomeokee, or "The Great Guide," Pilot Mountain is capped by vertical cliff walls rising to a forested dome known as Big Pinnacle. The peak has served as a navigational landmark for centuries, and even today it is a near-constant presence throughout the surrounding countryside. Big Pinnacle is closed to all public access for ecological and safety reasons, but the trail provides glimpses of its majesty.

The park's ecology is more similar to that in mountain environments such as the Blue Ridge Mountains than to the surrounding Piedmont. Plants like Catawba rhododendron and mountain laurel are common, and mountain tree species such as Table Mountain pine thrive.

Although there are more facilities and a visitor center at the park's main entrance, that area is extremely popular, and parking fills up early most weekends. When that happens, the main entrance is closed to all further vehicles. Therefore, we have recommended beginning this hike at the Pinnacle Hotel Rd. parking lot, which is rarely crowded.

The hike begins by crossing Pinnacle Hotel Rd. and following the co-located MST and Mountain Trail, which is marked with red blazes and white circles. Be sure not to follow the Grassy Ridge Trail, which intersects the road about 75 yards east.

The trail steadily climbs through fairly open woods for the first 1.5 miles, then remains generally level, with only minor ups and downs, for the next 2 miles or so.

At mile 3.5, the MST reaches an intersection with the Grindstone Trail. The MST and this hike continue to the left arm of the Grindstone Trail. The right arm continues up the mountain to a loop at the base of Big Pinnacle. In another 0.3 mile, after a short descent and ascent, the MST reaches the park campground and turns right. From here, the trail steadily descends, crossing the Pilot Creek Trail (which leads 3.3 miles to a trailhead on Boyd Nelson Rd.) and Pilot Knob Park Rd. At 4.7 miles, the trail reaches the park office; if space allows, a parking lot here can be used to shorten the hike.

Beyond the park office, the trail becomes known as the Grassy Ridge Trail. After 0.1 mile, this hike turns right onto the Mountain Trail, leaving the MST. One mile farther, the Mountain Trail branches; the left branch returns to the trailhead, completing the loop.

DRIVING DIRECTIONS

Pilot Mountain State Park is approximately 20 miles northwest of Winston-Salem. To reach the trailhead, take US 52 to exit 129, signed to Pinnacle. At the end of the exit ramp, turn right on Perch Rd. Travel 0.9 mile and turn left on Old US 52, then almost immediately turn left on Surry Line Rd. Stay on this road 1.7 miles to the trailhead, at the intersection with Culler Rd. (Surry Line Rd. becomes Pinnacle Hotel Rd. where it crosses under the US 52 overpass.)

HIKE DIRECTIONS

0.0   From the parking lot, go around a wooden fence, then cross Pinnacle Hotel Rd. and begin walking on the Mountain Trail, marked with red blazes and white circles. *Note*: Do not follow the Grassy Ridge Trail, which intersects the road about 75 yards east of the Mountain Trail.

0.5   At a T-intersection, turn left, following the sign to the campground.

2.1   Cross a small stream on a set of boulder steps.

3.5   Turn left at a trail crossing, following the MST sign onto the Grindstone Trail, marked with blue blazes as well as white blazes. Just before reaching a well pump house, turn right to continue on the trail.

3.7   Continue straight across a jeep road.

3.8   At the campground, turn right to stay on the trail.

4.2   Continue straight past the junction with the Pilot Creek Trail.

4.4   Cross Pilot Knob Park Rd. near a stone park building and continue on the driveway through a parking lot, turning right to stay on the trail.

4.7   Pass an information kiosk at a spur to the park office and continue onto the Grassy Ridge Trail.

4.8   Turn right onto the Mountain Trail, leaving the MST.

5.8   At the junction with the other end of the Mountain Trail loop, turn left to return to the trailhead.

6.3   Return to the trailhead.

SPECIAL CONSIDERATIONS

Pilot Mountain State Park is extremely popular, and the main parking lots fill to capacity and are closed to additional vehicles most weekends. Therefore, we have designed this hike as a loop beginning at the Pinnacle Hotel Rd. lot, which is rarely crowded.

The park is open from 7:00 A.M. to sunset March–November, and 8:00 A.M.–6:00 P.M. December–February. Outside those hours, there is no access to the headquarters parking lot.

FOR MORE INFORMATION

Pilot Mountain State Park: www.ncparks.gov/pilot-mountain-state-park

Pilot Mountain State Park Map (Mountain Section): files.nc.gov/ncparks /maps-and-brochures/pilot-mountain-state-park-map-mountain -section.pdf

Friends of the Sauratown Mountains (trail maintainers for this section): sauratownfriends.org

Hike 16

HANGING ROCK STATE PARK

Tory's Den Parking Lot to Hanging Rock Lake

The Sauratown Mountains and Pilot Mountain from Moore's Knob. Photo by Keith Sidden.

Distance: 5.3 miles one-way (5.1 miles on MST plus 0.2-mile spur to parking lot); 10.6 miles round-trip

Degree of difficulty: Moderate to strenuous

Trail type: Natural-surface trail

Trailhead 1: Tory's Den parking lot; no facilities

Trailhead 1 coordinates: N36.40167, W80.29990

Trailhead 1 elevation: 1,426 feet

Trailhead 2: Hanging Rock Lake parking lot; food, supplies, water, restrooms

Trailhead 2 coordinates: N36.39050, W80.26670

Trailhead 2 elevation: 1,729 feet

Total elevation change: gain, 1,564 feet; loss, 1,261 feet

MST segment: 7

Highlights: Great views; lake

Dogs: Allowed on leash

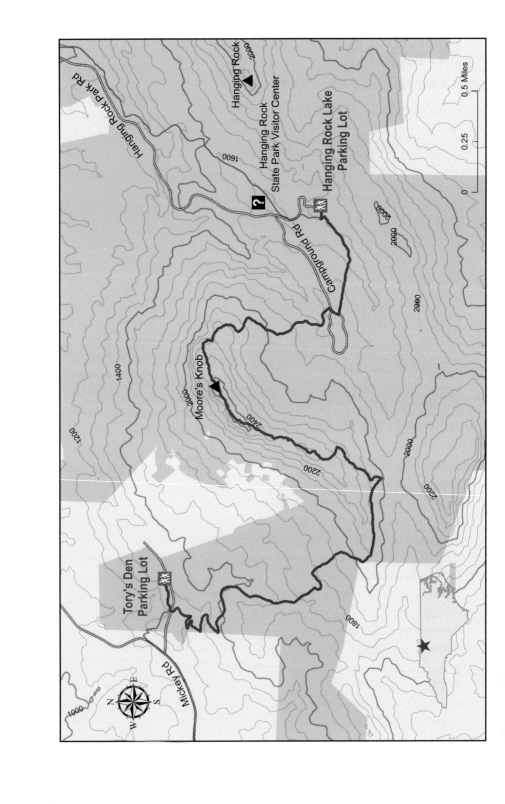

HIKE OVERVIEW

Situated in the Sauratown Mountains, the Piedmont's "Mountains away from the Mountains," this hike features great views, the chance of a little respite from summer heat, and swimming. Like Pilot Mountain to the west, the Sauratowns host plant communities that are more common in the Southern Appalachians than on the Piedmont. Rhododendron, mountain laurel, and galax are common, along with many other cooler-climate species. Nearly the entire hike is in Hanging Rock State Park, North Carolina's third-oldest state park.

The hike begins at Tory's Den parking lot, named for a nearby cave supposed to have been used by Tories as a hideout during the American Revolution. Another trail leads approximately 0.2 mile from the parking area to the cave and nearby falls.

From the back left corner of the parking lot, this hike follows a 0.2-mile spur trail, then turns left onto the MST and crosses Charlie Young Rd. From the trailhead at 1,400 feet, the trail climbs more than 1,000 feet in the next 2.9 miles to the ridgeline. Although steady, the climb is not overly taxing.

On the right at mile 0.9, the Ruben Mountain Trail offers a 3-mile-long alternative route for equestrians that rejoins the MST at mile 1.5. (Horses are not permitted beyond mile 1.5.) At mile 2.4, the trail joins the left half of the Moore's Wall Loop Trail, which is marked with red circles as well as the MST white circle.

At mile 3.6, the trail reaches a T-intersection. The hike continues to the right, but the left arm, leading a few yards to the summit of Moore's Knob, is a must-do. The lookout tower atop this 2,579-foot peak—the highest in the Sauratown Mountains—offers 360-degree vistas over the Piedmont, the Sauratowns, Pilot Mountain, and, in the distance, the Blue Ridge.

From Moore's Knob, the trail descends through oak-hickory forest to the end of the hike at Hanging Rock Lake, popular for swimming and boating in the summer. The lake features a bathhouse constructed in the 1930s by the Civilian Conservation Corps, which is now on the National Register of Historic Places. Open daily in the summer and on weekends in the spring and fall (generally from 10:00 A.M. to 5:30 or 5:45 P.M., although hours may vary), the bathhouse has drinks, water, and snacks for sale, as well as restrooms.

DRIVING DIRECTIONS

The trailheads are roughly 30 miles from Winston-Salem. To reach them, drive north on US 52 approximately 12 miles to exit 122, "Moore—RJR Drive." At the top of the exit ramp, turn left onto Moore—RJR Dr., following the sign to Hanging Rock State Park. The road soon changes its name to Moore Rd. and then, at the intersection with Old US 52, to Mountain View Rd. After a total of 4.3 miles on these roads, turn left on NC 66, still following signs to Hanging Rock State Park. Stay on NC 66 for 6.9 miles, then turn right on Moores Spring Rd., which again has a sign for Hanging Rock State Park.

To reach Trailhead 1, Tory's Den parking lot, continue 0.5 mile on Moores Spring Rd., then turn right on Mickey Rd. After another 0.8 mile, turn right on Charlie Young Rd. and follow it 0.4 mile to the parking lot on the left.

To reach Trailhead 2, Hanging Rock Lake, continue straight on Moores Spring Rd. past Mickey Rd. After a total of 5.5 miles, reach a T-intersection and turn right on State Park Rd. Follow this road 2.0 miles to the parking lot at the end.

HIKE DIRECTIONS

0.0 Head west on the trail from the back left corner of the Tory's Den parking lot.

0.2 At a T-intersection with a sign pointing to the lake parking area, turn left to cross Charlie Young Rd.

0.3 Cross a bridge over a creek.

0.9 Bear left at a Y-intersection just past blazed tree 78. *Note:* The right fork is the Ruben Mountain Trail, which goes 3.0 miles then rejoins this hike at mile 1.5.

1.5 Turn left at the sign for hikers only, to lake parking, continuing to follow blue circles and white circles.

2.4 At a sign reading "Parking Area 1.5 mi.," turn left onto the Moore's Wall Loop Trail, also marked with red circles.

3.6 At a T-intersection, turn right toward lake parking. *Note:* Turning left leads a few yards to Moore's Knob lookout tower, with fine vistas over the Piedmont, the Sauratown Mountains, Pilot Mountain, and, in the distance, the Blue Ridge.

4.6 Cross Cascade Creek, then continue up a set of stairs curving to the left.

4.7 Turn right on Campground Rd.

4.8 Turn left onto the trail at the sign for Moore's Wall Loop trailhead.

5.0 Bear left where a trail comes in from right, then bear right at a Y-intersection. Cross a footbridge and two wooden boardwalks.

5.3 Pass the trail to Cook's Wall on the right. At the bathhouse, turn right onto the driveway and reach the Hanging Rock Lake parking lot and the end of the hike.

FOR MORE INFORMATION

Hanging Rock State Park: www.ncparks.gov/hanging-rock-state-park

Hanging Rock State Park Map: files.nc.gov/ncparks/maps-and -brochures/hanging-rock-park-map.pdf

Sauratown Trails Association (trail maintainers for part of this hike): www.sauratowntrails.org

Friends of the Sauratown Mountains (trail maintainers for part of this hike): sauratownfriends.org

Hike 17
CASCADES PRESERVE LOOP

Waterfalls at Cascades Preserve. Photo by Jim Grode.

Distance: 2.0-mile loop (1.5 on MST, 0.5 on other trail)
Degree of difficulty: Easy
Trail type: Natural-surface trail
Trailhead: Cascades Preserve Trailhead; no facilities
Trailhead coordinates: N36.19479, W80.03090
Trailhead elevation: 859 feet
Total elevation change: gain, 268 feet; loss, 268 feet
MST segment: 8
Highlights: Mature Piedmont forest; wildflowers; waterfalls
Dogs: Allowed on leash

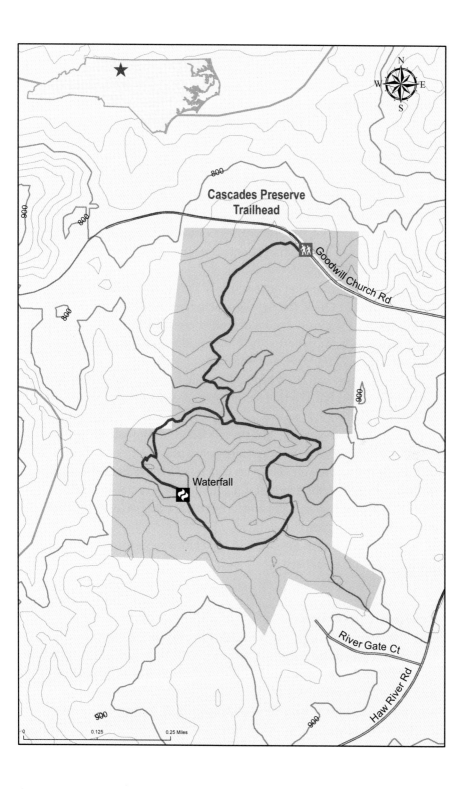

Cascades Preserve
Trailhead

Goodwill Church Rd

Waterfall

River Gate Ct

Haw River Rd

N
W E
S

800
900
800
800
900
900
900
900

0   0.125   0.25 Miles

HIKE OVERVIEW

Nestled close to the suburbs of Greensboro, the 130-acre Cascades Preserve, managed by the town of Oak Ridge, is a hidden gem. Mature hardwood forest provides a cool respite from the summer heat, and, in spring, wildflowers abound. This easy hike also contains a rarity: waterfalls in the heart of the central Piedmont. The hike forms a "lollipop," with a stem and loop. The loop can, of course, be hiked in either direction, but we recommend the direction described here (counterclockwise) because it is the better way to view the waterfalls.

From the parking lot, the hike crosses Goodwill Church Rd. to the trailhead. At mile 0.5, continue straight onto the right fork of the trail to begin the loop of the "lollipop."

At the next Y-intersection (mile 0.7), take the left fork to begin walking alongside Cascade Creek. The right fork here runs parallel to the creek on the other side. It rejoins the route described here at mile 1.0. It is slightly longer and provides an opportunity to add an additional loop, but does not have good views of the creek and waterfalls.

At mile 0.8, the waterfalls begin. There are benches and tables overlooking the lowest fall. The trail has additional views of falls for the next 0.2 mile.

At the next Y-intersection, take the left fork. The alternate route mentioned at mile 0.7 rejoins the route here from across the creek. Shortly beyond this junction the MST continues on a trail to the right, but this hike continues straight. A little farther is a potentially tricky trail intersection. A trail may appear to go straight ahead, but the correct trail switches back; it is marked with a blaze.

At the trail junction at mile 1.5, turn right onto the stem of the lollipop, leading back to the trailhead.

DRIVING DIRECTIONS

From the intersection of NC 68 and Oak Ridge Rd. (NC 150) in Oak Ridge, head southeast on Oak Ridge Rd. After 0.4 mile, turn right at the traffic light onto Linville Rd. Continue on Linville Rd. 2.5 miles to a T-intersection. Turn left onto Haw River Rd. After 0.2 mile, take the first right onto Goodwill Church Rd. Stay on Goodwill Church Rd. 0.6 mile to the trailhead parking lot on the right.

HIKE DIRECTIONS

0.0 Begin the hike from the parking lot by crossing Goodwill Church Rd., then going through a gate.

0.1 Pass a picnic table.

0.4 Cross a creek on a footbridge.

0.5 Cross a creek on a small footbridge, and take the right fork at the Falling Waters Trail sign immediately after.

0.7 At a Y-intersection, take the left fork.

0.8 Pass benches and tables overlooking cascades.

1.0 Pass a smaller cascade. At the next Y-intersection, take the left fork again. Continue straight past a trail on the right marked with a double MST blaze. The MST continues on the right-hand trail toward Haw River Rd., but this day hike leaves the MST here.

1.1 Turn left at a switchback. A trail appears to go straight, but the correct trail is marked with a blaze.

1.5 Turn right at the sign for Falling Waters Trail, then cross a creek on a small footbridge. You are now returning on the same trail you walked at the beginning of the hike.

1.6 Cross a creek on a footbridge.

2.0 Reach Goodwill Church Rd. and the end of the hike.

FOR MORE INFORMATION

Town of Oak Ridge: www.oakridgenc.com

Cascades Preserve: www.guilfordcountync.gov/our-county/county
-parks/passive-parks/cascades-preserve

Cascades Preserve Map: www.guilfordcountync.gov/home/show
document?id=3097

Hike 18

GREENSBORO WATERSHED LAKES

Lake Brandt Marina to Church Street

The Laurel Bluff Trail,
Greensboro Watershed lakes.
Photo by Greg Yahn.

Distance: 3.5 miles one-way (3.4 miles on MST plus 0.1-mile spur);
7.0 miles round-trip
Degree of difficulty: Easy to moderate
Trail type: Natural-surface trail
Trailhead 1: Lake Brandt Marina; food, water, restrooms
Trailhead 1 coordinates: N36.16740, W79.83695
Trailhead 1 elevation: 771 feet
Trailhead 2: Church St. parking lot; no facilities
Trailhead 2 coordinates: N36.17396, W79.79207
Trailhead 2 elevation: 741 feet
Total elevation change: gain, 401 feet; loss, 430 feet
MST segment: 8
Highlights: Lake views; wildflowers; mature Piedmont forest
Dogs: Allowed on leash

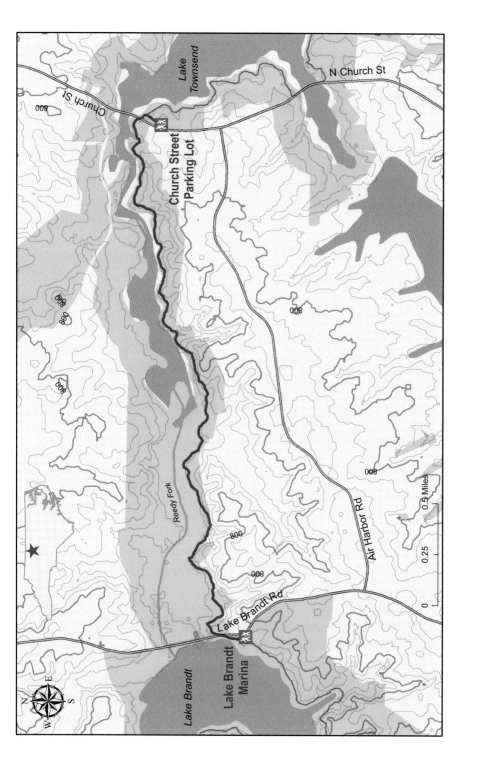

Lake Townsend

N Church St

Church St

800

Church Street
Parking Lot

800

Reedy Fork

800

800

800

800

Air Harbor Rd

0   0.25   0.5 Miles

Lake Brandt Rd

Lake Brandt

Lake Brandt
Marina

N
W   E
S

HIKE OVERVIEW

The Greensboro Watershed Lakes are a string of three lakes—Higgins, Brandt, and Townsend—that provide water to the city of Greensboro. Nearly 50 miles of trails surround the lakes, offering bountiful opportunities for hiking, running, biking, and nature watching. The MST incorporates 19 miles of these trails, mostly along the southern shores of Lake Brandt and Lake Townsend. This hike, also known as the Laurel Bluff Trail, is on one of the most scenic, and relatively little-used, sections of the trail. Mainly passing through mature second-growth hardwood forest, it features a wide variety of wildflowers and wildlife, along with great views of the lake.

The hike begins at the Lake Brandt Marina, which has water, restrooms, drinks, and snacks (operating hours vary seasonally). Just inside the fence, the trail turns left from the access road. After crossing Lake Brandt Rd. at the crosswalk (use care here), the hike joins the Laurel Bluff Trail and soon passes an old tobacco barn.

The trail continues, mainly through the woods, to Church St., which should be crossed with extreme care. On the other side of the road, the trail becomes the Crockett Trail, named in honor of Pat Crockett, who was killed while trying to cross the road here. Just past the crossing, turn right onto the white-diamond-blazed trail to the parking lot and the end of the hike.

DRIVING DIRECTIONS

To reach Trailhead 1, Lake Brandt Marina, from Greensboro, head northwest on US 220 (Battleground Ave.). Just before reaching I-73, turn right on Cotswold Ave., which will become Lake Brandt Rd. After 1.9 miles, turn left at the traffic light to remain on Lake Brandt Rd. The trailhead is 1.1 miles ahead on the left.

To reach Trailhead 2, Church St. parking lot, head north from Greensboro on Elm St. Turn right on Pisgah Church Rd. In 0.5 mile, turn left at the traffic light onto N. Church St., which will become just Church St. The trailhead is 2.9 miles ahead on the left.

To shuttle between the trailheads, head south on Lake Brandt Rd. (from Trailhead 1) or Church St. (from Trailhead 2) to the first traffic light at Air Harbor Rd. Turn left (from Trailhead 1) or right (from Trailhead 2) and follow Air Harbor Rd. to its end, in either case turning back to the north and continuing to the trailhead. If you're coming from Trailhead 1, be sure to keep left at the Y-intersection to stay on Air Harbor Rd. after 0.5 mile.

HIKE DIRECTIONS

0.0 From the parking area, head out Lake Brandt Marina Rd. toward Lake Brandt Rd., then turn left on the trail.

0.1 Cross a bridge (with no railing), then go through an opening in the fence. Cross Lake Brandt Rd. at the crosswalk, then turn left. In about 200 feet, turn right on the Laurel Bluff Trail.

0.2 Turn right at the trail sign.

0.3 Turn left at a trail sign by an old tobacco barn.

0.4 Cross a footbridge, then cross a natural gas pipeline right-of-way.

0.8 Cross two footbridges.

1.4 Cross two footbridges.

1.5 Cross a footbridge.

2.0 Cross a small unbridged stream.

3.2 Cross a footbridge.

3.4 Cross Church St. and continue onto the Crockett (formerly Peninsula) Trail, then turn right on the trail blazed with a white diamond.

3.5 Pass through a gap in the fence to reach the parking area and the end of the hike.

SPECIAL CONSIDERATIONS

Use extreme caution crossing Church St., which is narrow, curvy, and heavily traveled and has been the site of a fatal pedestrian crash.

If the gate at the Lake Brandt Marina, Trailhead 1, is locked or if you will be returning after hours, you can park in the gravel area outside the fence and walk along the road to the trail. Hours vary seasonally and are posted at the entrance.

FOR MORE INFORMATION

Greensboro Watershed Trails Guide: www.greensboro-nc.gov/modules /showdocument.aspx?documentid=3194

Greensboro Watershed Lakes: www.greensboro-nc.gov/index.aspx ?page=1372

Hike 19

THE HAW RIVER TRAIL

Great Bend Park to Stoney Creek Marina

Historic Glencoe Mill Village. Photo by Jim Grode.

Distance: 2.9 miles one-way; 5.8 miles round-trip
Degree of difficulty: Moderate
Trail type: Natural-surface trail
Trailhead 1: Great Bend Park; restrooms
Trailhead 1 coordinates: N36.14368, W79.43333
Trailhead 1 elevation: 564 feet
Trailhead 2: Stoney Creek Marina; no facilities
Trailhead 2 coordinates: N36.12694, W79.40637
Trailhead 2 elevation: 555 feet
Total elevation change: gain, 244 feet; loss, 253 feet
MST segment: 9
Highlights: Beautiful trail along the rocky Haw River; historic textile mill and village
Dogs: Allowed on leash

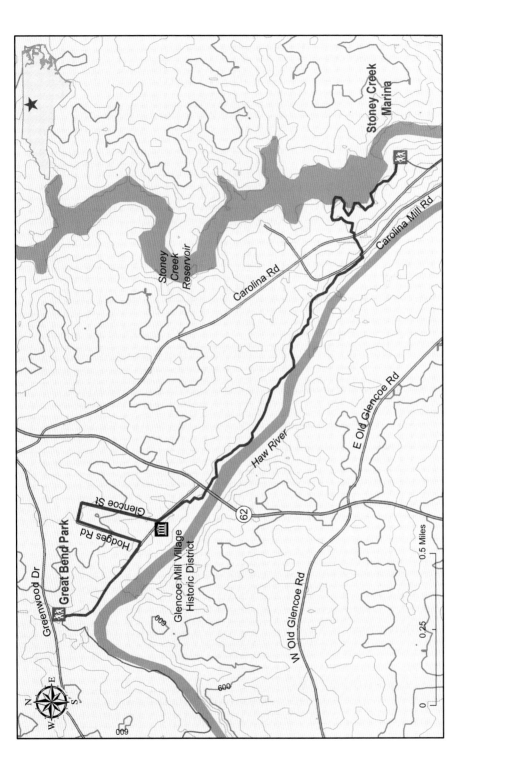

Stoney Creek
Marina

Carolina Mill Rd

Carolina Rd

Stoney
Creek
Reservoir

E Old Glencoe Rd

Haw River

Glencoe St

Hodges Rd

Great Bend Park

Greenwood Dr

Glencoe Mill Village
Historic District

W Old Glencoe Rd

62

600

600

600

0   0.25   0.5 Miles

HIKE OVERVIEW

This trail captures a slice of one of the most important economic engines in the Piedmont of the nineteenth and early twentieth centuries: textiles. From the rapidly flowing, rocky river that provided the power, to the village where the mill workers lived, to the mills that produced the textiles, you will encounter the full range of the industry. In between, enjoy the beautiful woods, wildlife, and nature sounds along this diverse stretch.

From the Great Bend Park parking lot, the trail goes down into a field and turns left at a T-intersection. After a couple of hundred yards, it reaches the banks of the Haw River and begins heading downstream.

The trail soon passes a paddle access and the 0.5-mile-long Island Trail. The side trail here crosses over the head of an old mill race (which forms the island for which the trail is named) and overlooks the dam that provided water used by the Glencoe Cotton Mill, the three-story Italianate mill just downstream, to generate power.

About 250 yards farther, the trail reaches the Glencoe Mill and Mill Village Historic District. Many of the historic mill buildings and homes in the village, which dates from the 1880s, have been painstakingly restored and have found new owners and modern uses. The main mill offices and company store are now the Textile Heritage Museum, which showcases life in Carolina mill towns from the late 1800s through the 1950s and includes artifacts including a loom and knitting machines as well as mill and company store products (open 9:00 A.M.–5:00 P.M., Tuesday–Saturday; closed on major holidays). There is also an artists' studio in the village.

After going through the streets of the village, the MST returns to the Haw River Trail, which takes on a more natural feel as it meanders through woods along the banks of the Haw. After a mile of serene walking with few signs of human development, it passes behind an old mill building, then crosses two roads in succession. A short but moderately steep climb here leads to the shores of Stoney Creek Reservoir. After another 0.5 mile meandering along the curves of the lake, the trail reaches the marina and the end of the hike.

DRIVING DIRECTIONS

From Burlington, head north on NC 62 (Rauhut St.). To reach Trailhead 1, cross the Haw River, then, after 0.6 mile, turn left at the traffic light onto Union Ridge Rd. After just a couple of hundred yards, take the first left onto

Greenwood Dr. Continue another 0.6 mile to the entrance to Great Bend Park on the left.

To reach Trailhead 2, go through the traffic light at NC 62 and Sharpe Rd., then take the next right onto Lower Hopedale Rd. Continue 1.4 miles, crossing the Haw River, to a T-intersection. Turn right here onto Carolina Mill Rd., then after 0.2 mile take the first left on Carolina Rd. After another 0.2 mile, turn right onto Faulkner Rd., the driveway for the Stoney Creek Marina. At the end of the driveway, there are a few parking spaces for hikers.

To shuttle between the trailheads, return toward Burlington and, after crossing the river, take the first significant left (if coming from Great Bend Park) or right (if coming from Stoney Creek Marina) onto E. Old Glencoe Rd. After 0.7 mile, turn back toward the river and follow the remaining directions to the other trailhead.

HIKE DIRECTIONS

0.0 To begin the hike, follow the trail next to the restroom into the woods. After about 25 yards, turn left at a T-intersection.

0.2 Continue straight along the old roadbed past a paddle-access area with a picnic table and Island Trail on the right. Pass a gate and continue straight on Mill Race Rd. You are entering the restored historic mill town of Glencoe.

0.4 Turn left on Hodges Rd.

0.6 Turn right on Sarah Rhyne Rd.

0.7 Turn right on Glencoe St.

0.9 Turn slightly left on Glencoe St. past the village water tank on the left.

1.1 Turn right on the Haw River Trail and follow the trail through woods.

1.2 Cross a parking lot and continue on the trail past the Glencoe Paddle Access and under NC 62.

2.1 After two sets of steps, enter an open area behind a mill building. The trail goes behind the building and follows telephone poles paralleling Carolina Mill Rd.

2.2 Turn left on the trail to cross Carolina Mill Rd., then Carolina Rd.

2.9 At a kiosk, turn right past the Haw River Trail / MST signboard and continue on the stone path along the chain-link fence to the entrance gate to Stoney Creek Marina and the end of the hike.

FOR MORE INFORMATION

MST / Haw River Trail segment: www.thehaw.org/land-trail/land-trail
-maps/glencoe-sellers-falls

Glencoe Mill Village and Textile Heritage Museum:
textileheritagemuseum.org

Glencoe Studios, Art in Action: glencoestudios.com

Haw River Trail: www.thehaw.org/land-trail/land-trail-overview

Hike 20
HILLSBOROUGH'S RIVERWALK
Gold Park to Occoneechee Speedway

Eno River bridge on Hillsborough's Riverwalk. Photo by Jim Grode.

Distance: 2.1 miles one-way; 4.2 miles round-trip
Degree of difficulty: Easy
Trail type: Paved greenway and natural-surface trail
Trailhead 1: Gold Park; water, restrooms
Trailhead 1 coordinates: N36.07057, W79.11031
Trailhead 1 elevation: 511 feet
Trailhead 2: Historic Occoneechee Speedway Trail; no facilities
Trailhead 2 coordinates: N36.07132, W79.08159
Trailhead 2 elevation: 504 feet
Total elevation change: gain, 101 feet; loss, 108 feet
MST segment: 9
Highlights: Lovely greenway along the Eno River; historic trail town; historic NASCAR speedway
Dogs: Allowed on leash

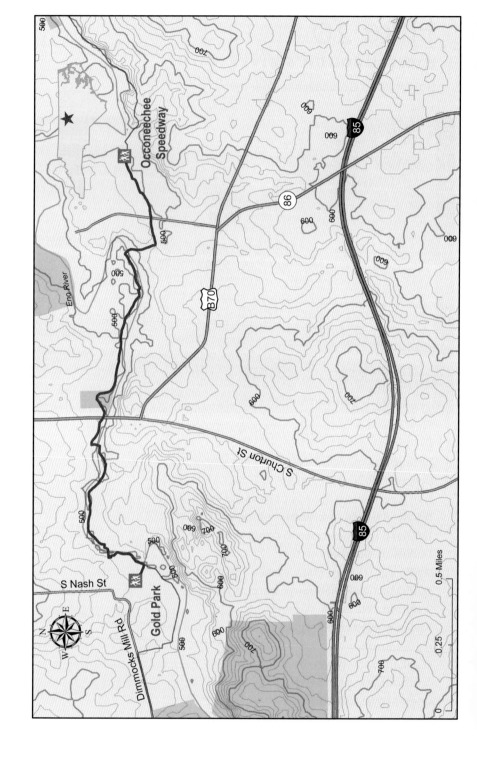

HIKE OVERVIEW

Hillsborough is one of the most historic towns in North Carolina. At the heart of the 1765–71 Regulator uprising against the British leading up to the Revolutionary War, it was later home to the North Carolina legislature during the war itself. This hike passes along the Eno River to the center of this bustling town. Turning to more recent history, the hike continues to the Occoneechee Speedway, one of the first two NASCAR racetracks to open in the inaugural 1949 season. Numerous informational panels along the trail provide a wealth of information about the area's history and ecology.

The hike begins on the sidewalk through the open area of Gold Park, passing to the left of the dog park. Water and restrooms are available at the trailhead May–September. Just before reaching the Eno River, considered one of the most important ecological areas in the Triangle, the route turns left onto the MST and Hillsborough's Riverwalk, a paved greenway.

Leaving Gold Park, the path passes a pollinator garden, then crosses under the railroad tracks on a walkway that is covered for protection from train debris. Just before reaching a bridge over the Eno, the path turns right. Turning left here instead leads to Calvin St., where another left turn leads to the restaurants of West End Hillsborough. Just past the bridge, the MST turns left; the trail straight ahead forms part of the Peggy Cates Bartow Loop, named for an early champion of the Riverwalk who donated some of the land for the trail. The loop returns to the MST after 0.2 mile.

The path continues meandering along the south bank of the Eno for 0.4 mile until reaching a sharp left turn. It then crosses the Eno again and turns right on a boardwalk. Continuing straight ahead instead takes hikers to the shops, historic sites, and restaurants of historic downtown Hillsborough.

The MST crosses under Exchange Park Ln. and Churton St., entering River Park. In River Park, side paths lead to the Eno River Farmers Market, open Saturdays 8:00 A.M.–noon April–November, 10:00 A.M.–noon December–March.

The trail continues past the Occaneechi Village Replica Site, a reconstructed seventeenth-century Native American village. At mile 1.5, the trail enters historic Ayr Mount Plantation, a Classical American Homes Preservation Trust property. (The early nineteenth-century plantation house itself is some distance away from the MST.) The trail then crosses the river on a bridge donated by Classical American Homes.

Continuing past the Vietri outlet store and across Elizabeth Brady Rd., the trail comes to the Historic Occoneechee Speedway Trail. Parking and the trailhead are at the road, but it is worthwhile to continue another quarter mile or so to see the historic racetrack. Beyond Elizabeth Brady Rd., the forest becomes much thicker and noticeably quieter than it was previously. Although most of the speedway area is now forested, the grandstands and much of the old dirt track are still visible, along with the remains of several other structures.

DRIVING DIRECTIONS

To reach Trailhead 1, Gold Park, from downtown Hillsborough, head west five blocks on King St., then turn left on S. Nash St. (signed to Gold Park and the Riverwalk). Continue two blocks, until the road curves 90 degrees to the right, then bear left onto Dimmocks Mill Rd. The entrance to Gold Park is on the left just after the railroad bridge.

To reach Trailhead 2, Occoneechee Speedway, from downtown Hillsborough, head south on Churton St. After crossing the Eno River, take the first left onto NC 86 (signed to the Speedway Trail). Continue on this road 0.8 mile, then turn left on Elizabeth Brady Rd., still following signs to the Speedway Trail. The entrance to the parking lot is 0.3 mile ahead on the right.

HIKE DIRECTIONS

0.0 From the parking lot at Gold Park, walk on the paved trail to the left of the pavilion and the dog park.

0.1 At the T-intersection, turn left onto the Hillsborough Riverwalk.

0.2 Pass a path and pollinator garden on the left, then cross under railroad tracks on covered walkway.

0.3 At the T-intersection, turn right to cross a bridge over the Eno River, then turn left immediately past the bridge, where the trail straight ahead is the Peggy Cates Bartow Loop.

0.5 Continue straight past the other end of the Peggy Cates Bartow Loop on the right.

0.7 Continue past a path to Faribault Ln. on the right and a picnic table on the left.

0.8 Cross a bridge over the Eno River and then turn right onto a boardwalk.

0.9 Cross under the Exchange Park Ln. bridge and continue straight onto the paved trail. Continue under the Churton St. bridge, then enter River Park and stay on the paved trail.

1.0 Pass a side path on the left leading to Eno River Farmers Market, cross a small footbridge over a creek, then continue past another path to the market. Pass the Occaneechi Village Replica Site on the right.

1.1 Leave River Park, staying on the paved trail paralleling the Eno River.

1.3 Cross a bridge over a low area that carries water in wet periods, then continue onto the gravel trail.

1.5 Enter historic Ayr Mount Plantation, a Classical American Homes Preservation Trust property.

1.6 Cross the Eno River.

1.7 Turn left by the Vietri outlet store to stay on the trail.

1.9 Cross Elizabeth Brady Rd. and continue through the Historic Occoneechee Speedway Trail parking lot past a kiosk and onto the trail toward the historic racetrack.

2.0 After the trail makes a sharp left turn, bear right onto the main access road.

2.1 At the end of the road, reach a kiosk with a map of the Historic Occoneechee Speedway Trail on the left and the end of this day hike. Retrace your steps to parking, or continue on to the speedway.

FOR MORE INFORMATION

Hillsborough's Riverwalk: www.hillsboroughnc.gov/community/park
-facilities/riverwalk

Hillsborough's Riverwalk Map: assets.hillsboroughnc.gov/media
/documents/public/riverwalk-and-mountains-to-sea-trail-network
-map.pdf

To purchase a beautifully detailed map of the Eno River trails from the Hillsborough Riverwalk to Old Oxford Hwy. near Penny's Bend: artshikingmaps.info

Historic Occoneechee Speedway Trail: www.visitnc.com/listing/historic
-occoneechee-speedway-trail

Historic Speedway Group: www.historicspeedwaygroup.org

Classical American Homes / Ayr Mount: classicalamericanhomes.org
/ayr-mount

Hike 21

THE ENO RIVER *Cabe Lands to Pump Station*

Dam ruins on Nancy Rhodes Creek near the Eno River. Photo by Bill Boyarsky.

Distance: Three options—(1) 3.5 miles one-way (2.9 miles on MST, plus
   two spur trails, one 0.2 mile long and one 0.4 mile long); 7.0 miles
   round-trip; (2) 4.4 (3.5 miles on MST, plus two spur trails, one 0.2 mile
   long and one 0.7 mile long); 8.8 miles round-trip; or (3) 1.7-mile loop
Degree of difficulty: Moderate
Trail type: Natural-surface trail
Trailhead 1: Cabe Lands Access on Howe St.; no facilities
Trailhead 1 coordinates: N36.03975, W78.99065
Trailhead 1 elevation: 489 feet
Trailhead 2: Pump Station Access on Rivermont Rd.; no facilities
Trailhead 2 coordinates: N36.05886, W78.96909
Trailhead 2 elevation: 423 feet
Total elevation change: gain, 398 feet; loss, 463 feet
MST segment: 10
Highlights: River views; bluffs; spring wildflowers; pump station ruins
Dogs: Allowed on leash

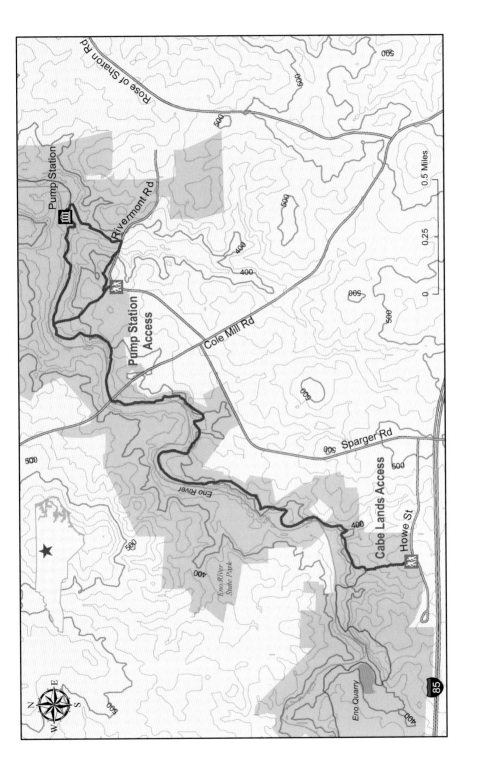

Pump Station

Rose of Sharon Rd

Rivermont Rd

Pump Station Access

Cole Mill Rd

Sparger Rd

Cabe Lands Access

Howe St

Eno River

Eno River State Park

Eno Quarry

85

500

500

500

500

500

500

500

500

500

500

400

400

400

400

400

N
W   E
S

0   0.25   0.5 Miles

HIKE OVERVIEW

The Eno River rises in Orange County and joins with the Flat River to become the Neuse and empty into Falls Lake. Named after the Eno people, who lived here before European arrival, the river is a swift and mostly shallow stream. Much of the river, including the area of this hike, is protected in Eno River State Park.

The MST runs along the banks of the Eno for some 22 miles, more than half the river's length. This hike is in probably the most varied stretch along the river, with bluffs and rocky coves that give it a mountainous feel, mature woods and meadows, and former industrial and homesites. This book describes two options for the eastern end of the hike as well as a shorter loop option combining the two eastern options.

Leaving from the back left corner of the parking lot on Howe St., the hike begins descending on the Cabe Lands Trail (not part of the MST proper, and marked with red dots). This area is named for Barnaby Cabe, a British loyalist who owned property here before the American Revolution.

The trail soon passes the blue-blazed Eno Quarry Trail on the left. This trail leads approximately 0.7 mile to an old quarry that is a popular swimming spot in the summer and a scenic spot any time of year. If you choose to follow this trail to the quarry, you can return along the river on the MST to resume the hike at mile 0.2 rather than backtracking to this point.

At mile 0.2, the hike turns right onto the MST, also known as the Laurel Bluffs Trail (blazed with yellow dots as well as white MST circles). The trail in this section has several short but steep climbs in and out of coves, with many fine views of the river from atop high bluffs or along the banks.

At mile 0.7, the MST passes a plaque honoring Ann Zener, a local woman instrumental in preserving the Eno River from multiple threats. Shortly after the plaque, the trail reaches the river for the first time, then passes the remains of an old homesite.

At mile 2.3 are more ruins, this time of a small stone water-pump house. A bit later, Cole Mill Rd. passes overhead. This stretch of the river has several sets of small rapids.

At mile 3.1, the trail reaches a junction with the Pump Station Trail, marked with red blazes. There are two options here. For the first, shorter option, turn right; for the second, longer option, continue straight. The second option leads to the ruins of the former Durham water-supply pump station and a related dam, as well as a meadow with great spring wildflowers.

A third option for those seeking a shorter hike is to start at Trailhead 2 and combine the ends of the first two options into a single 1.7-mile loop from Rivermont Rd. For this option, begin by following the last 0.4 mile of Option 1 in reverse, then turn right on the MST and begin following Option 2.

DRIVING DIRECTIONS

To reach the trailheads, take exit 170 from I-85 onto US 70 East. If traveling south on I-85, exit to US 70 West, then make a U-turn at the first light. Go 1.8 miles on US 70, then turn left at the traffic light onto Sparger Rd. In 0.4 mile, cross over I-85.

To reach Trailhead 1, Cabe Lands Access, turn left just beyond I-85 onto Howe St., then go 0.5 mile to the parking area on the right.

To reach Trailhead 2, Pump Station Access, continue straight past Howe St. for another 1.3 miles to a T-intersection at Cole Mill Rd. Turn right, then immediately turn left on Rivermont Rd. After 0.8 mile, just after the pavement ends and at the beginning of a long curve, the parking area is at a wide spot in the road.

HIKE DIRECTIONS

0.0 From the back left corner of the parking lot, head downhill on the Cabe Lands Trail (marked with red dots) to begin the hike. Continue straight past the junction with the Eno Quarry Trail on the left.

0.2 At a trail junction, turn right onto the Laurel Bluffs Trail / MST (marked with yellow blazes and white circles).

0.4 Pass an unmarked trail on the right, which goes 0.3 mile to the Howe St. lot. After a short descent, pass another unmarked path going down to the river.

0.5 Cross a small creek on a footbridge. Ascend and traverse a laurel thicket as the trail narrows. The river can be seen and heard below.

0.7 Pass a plaque honoring Ann Zener, an Eno River preservationist, as the trail begins a descent from the ridgeline.

0.8 Reach the Eno and turn right to walk beside it. Cross a small creek on a footbridge, then begin ascending and pass the remains of Sparger Lodge.

1.1 Cross a small creek on a footbridge.

1.6 Pass a sign marking the Durham County line.

2.0 Cross a small creek on a footbridge.

2.3 Reach the river and turn right to walk beside it. Cross a small creek on a footbridge. To the right are the remains of a small stone water-pump house. Some rapids are to your left.

2.5 Walk under Cole Mill Rd. and pass by some rapids.

2.7 Near the river, cross a footbridge over a small creek and start to ascend, passing through some more laurel.

2.9 Continue through a power-line cut.

3.1 Reach a junction with the red-blazed Pump Station Trail. You have two options here. For the first, shorter option, turn right and follow the "Option 1" directions below. For the second, longer option, which includes views of the ruins of the former pump station, continue straight and follow the "Option 2" directions below.

OPTION 1

3.1 Turn right on the Pump Station Trail, which ascends gently to the parking area.

3.3 Continue through a power-line cut.

3.4 Continue straight past a trail junction on the left.

3.5 Reach the parking lot on Rivermont Rd. and the end of this hike.

OPTION 2

3.1 Continue straight at the intersection with the Pump Station Trail. The trail will continue through a basin known for its spring wildflower display.

3.6 Cross Nancy Rhodes Creek on a footbridge near the remains of a dam that once fed the pump station.

3.7 Cross another small footbridge and pass the ruins of the pump station (former Durham water supply). At the next trail junction, turn right to remain on the red-blazed Pump Station Trail.

3.9 Continue through a power-line cut.

4.1 Turn right on Rivermont Rd. at a small parking pullout, then cross a bridge over Nancy Rhodes Creek. Return to the woods trail at the other end of the bridge.

4.3 At a T-intersection, turn left.

4.4 Reach the parking lot on Rivermont Rd. and the end of this hike.

SPECIAL CONSIDERATIONS

Parking at both trailheads is limited and can fill up quite quickly, especially on summer weekends.

FOR MORE INFORMATION

Eno River Association: www.enoriver.org

Eno River State Park Trails Map: files.nc.gov/ncparks/maps-and
-brochures/eno-river-trails-map.pdf

To purchase a beautifully detailed map of the Eno River trails from the Hillsborough Riverwalk to Old Oxford Hwy. near Penny's Bend: artshikingmaps.info

Hike 22

THE FALLS LAKE TRAIL

Rolling View State Recreation Area to Little Lick Creek

Falls Lake at Little Lick Creek. Photo by Betsy Brown.

Distance: 4.5 miles one-way (4.0 miles on MST plus 0.5-mile spur);
    9.0 miles round-trip
Degree of difficulty: Moderate
Trail type: Natural-surface trail
Trailhead 1: Baptist Rd. hiker's lot; no facilities
Trailhead 1 coordinates: N36.00416, W78.72827
Trailhead 1 elevation: 347 feet
Trailhead 2: Little Lick Creek Bridge; no facilities
Trailhead 2 coordinates: N36.01119, W78.76960
Trailhead 2 elevation: 243 feet
Total elevation change: gain, 461 feet; loss, 566 feet
MST segment: 10
Highlights: Lake views; bluffs; mature Piedmont forest
Dogs: Allowed on leash

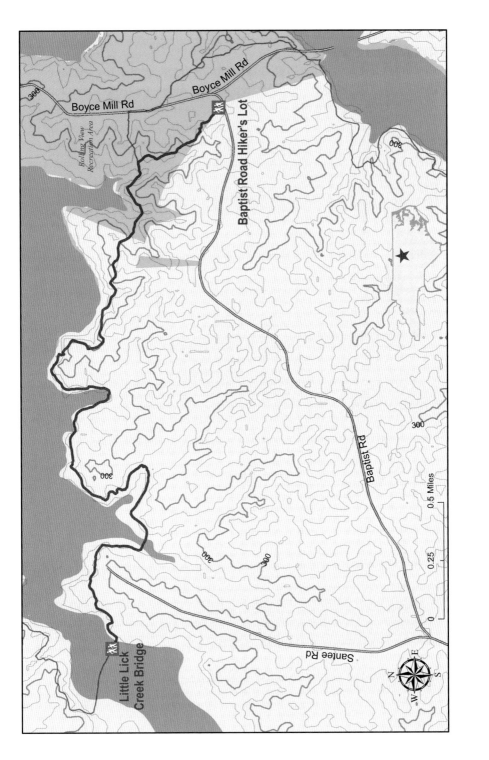

Boyce Mill Rd

Boyce Mill Rd

Boyce Mill Rd

Rolling View
Recreation Area

Baptist Road Hiker's Lot

300

300

300

300

300

Baptist Rd

300

Little Lick
Creek Bridge

Santee Rd

0.5 Miles

0.25

0

N
W E
S

HIKE OVERVIEW

This hike, part of the Falls Lake Trail running nearly the entire southern shore of Falls Lake, encompasses typical Piedmont and Falls Lake landscapes—gently rolling hills, second-growth pine and hardwood forests, various signs of the area's agricultural past—with a few twists. There are a few short but steep ascents and descents more reminiscent of the Appalachians than of the eastern Piedmont; the forest is more mature than is typical in this area; and there are some unusually panoramic views of Falls Lake, especially from atop a bluff near the midpoint of the hike and from the bridge at the end of the hike.

From the Baptist Rd. parking lot, the hike begins on the blue-blazed trail at the back of the lot. This spur trail descends for 0.5 mile to the MST, where this hike goes left.

At mile 0.9, the trail crosses an old roadbed, leaving state park lands and entering North Carolina Wildlife Game Lands. Hunting is allowed on the game lands, so if you are hiking during the hunting season, you should wear blaze orange for safety. (See "Special Considerations" to learn more about hunting in the area.)

At mile 1.3, the trail crosses a creek on the rock face at the lip of a small waterfall—much less daunting than it sounds! The next half mile or so includes a few climbs and descents and several lake views, the most notable of which is from the top of a bluff close to some private residences at mile 1.8. The MST here is very close to private property, so please stay on the trail.

Beyond the residences, the route returns to a more typical Piedmont landscape. At mile 2.9, note the horse pasture on the left. At mile 3.7, the trail emerges to a gravel road for a short stretch, then returns to the woods. A power-line cut at mile 4.3 signals that the hike is near an end.

After another 0.2 mile, the trail reaches a gravel road at another power line and turns right to begin crossing the Little Lick Creek arm of Falls Lake. The hike ends at the midpoint of the bridge. The bridge and boardwalk just to its west are good places to spot wading birds and waterfowl, who find good feeding in the arm's shallow waters.

From the end of the hike, hikers can return to Baptist Rd. or continue straight ahead to reach parking at Jimmy Rogers Rd.

DRIVING DIRECTIONS

To reach the trailheads, take NC 98 east from Durham or west from Creed-moor Rd. in northern Raleigh.

For Trailhead 1, the Baptist Rd. hiker's lot, turn north (left if coming from Durham) on Baptist Rd. Coming from Durham, this intersection is 0.7 mile after the traffic light at the intersection with Patterson and Sherron Rds. From Raleigh, it is 5.5 miles from Creedmoor Rd. After making the turn, continue straight on Baptist Rd. 4.0 miles to the parking area on the left just before the road makes a 90-degree left turn.

For Trailhead 2, turn north from NC 98 onto Patterson Rd. After 2.7 miles, turn right on Jimmy Rogers Rd. Continue 0.4 mile to a 90-degree left turn where Jimmy Rogers Rd. and Little Rogers Rd. meet; parking is in a gravel pullout on the outside of this turn.

HIKE DIRECTIONS

0.0 Take the blue-blazed trail at the back of the Baptist Rd. parking lot to begin the hike.

0.5 At the T-intersection, turn left onto the MST.

0.7 Cross one creek bed and soon another one in a low-lying area.

0.9 Cross an old roadbed, leaving state park lands at the North Carolina Wildlife Game Lands marker.

1.3 Cross a small creek on top of a rock face, then ascend slightly to some lake views.

1.8 Near the lakeshore, turn left to walk up steps to the top of a bluff overlooking the lake. Pass by some private residences as the trail narrows.

2.0 Pass through a slightly open area with lake views, which will continue for a short distance as the MST starts to move away from the lake.

2.2 Bear right and start to parallel a gravel road. Cross below the opening of a drainage pipe, then turn right and leave the road.

2.7 Cross a roadbed, which comes from a residence. Start to walk by the lakeshore, eventually crossing a faint path from another residence.

2.9 Head left, away from the lake shore, and then right to parallel a horse pasture.

3.1 Cross an overgrown roadbed.

3.2 Cross another overgrown roadbed, then two small creeks.

3.3 Cross a small channelized creek, then an overgrown roadbed.

3.5 Pass trail signage, then stay to the right by a residence. Start to walk near the lakeshore.

3.7 Turn right on a gravel road. Pass by a small pond on the left, then head right to reenter the woods.

4.1 Cross a narrow path, then go over another roadbed.

4.3 Pass by a small pond, then cross under a power line.

4.5 At another power line and gravel road, turn right to begin crossing the Little Lick Creek arm of Falls Lake on a large footbridge and boardwalk. The hike officially ends at the midpoint of the bridge. To finish, either retrace your steps to Baptist Rd. or continue straight across the bridge and boardwalk and onto an old roadbed leading 0.5 mile to Jimmy Rogers Rd.

SPECIAL CONSIDERATIONS

Parts of this trail are on thin slices of public land very close to private property. It is important to stay on the trail to maintain good relations with adjacent owners.

Hunting is allowed on game lands in Durham and Wake Counties by Falls Lake, including most of this hike except for the first 0.9 mile. When you are on the trail around Falls Lake, assume you are on game lands unless the book or signs state otherwise. Hunting is prohibited on Sunday. You can find more information about hunting seasons and the Butner–Falls of Neuse Game Land at www.ncwildlife.org/Hunting.

Parking at Jimmy Rogers Rd. is very limited, with room for only two to four vehicles.

FOR MORE INFORMATION

Falls Lake Map: files.nc.gov/ncparks/maps-and-brochures/falls-lake -state-recreation-area-map.pdf

Butner–Falls of Neuse Game Land Map: www.ncwildlife.org/Portals/0 /Hunting/Game-Land-Maps/Piedmont/Butner-Falls-of-Neuse.pdf

To purchase a beautifully detailed map of the Falls Lake Trail from Old Oxford Hwy. near Penny's Bend on the Eno River to Falls Lake dam: artshikingmaps.info

US Army Corps of Engineers at Falls Lake: www.saw.usace.army.mil /Locations/DistrictLakesandDams/FallsLake.aspx

Falls Lake State Recreation Area: www.ncparks.gov/falls-lake-state
-recreation-area
Geologic guide for Falls Lake: www.ncgeology.com/falls_lake_geology
/pages/TrailGuide_FallsLake_home.html

Hike 23

FALL LINE GEOLOGY

Raven Ridge Road to Falls Lake Dam Spillway

Typical Falls Lake trail view. Photo by Betsy Brown.

Distance: 3.5 miles one-way; 7.0 miles round-trip
Degree of difficulty: Moderate
Trail type: Natural-surface trail
Trailhead 1: Raven Ridge Rd. parking area; no facilities
Trailhead 1 coordinates: N35.92865, W78.60594
Trailhead 1 elevation: 283 feet
Trailhead 2: Tailrace Fishing Area parking lot; water, restrooms
Trailhead 2 coordinates: N35.93982, W78.58098
Trailhead 2 elevation: 222 feet
Total elevation change: gain, 424 feet; loss, 486 feet
MST segment: 10
Highlights: Lake views; geological interest
Dogs: Allowed on leash

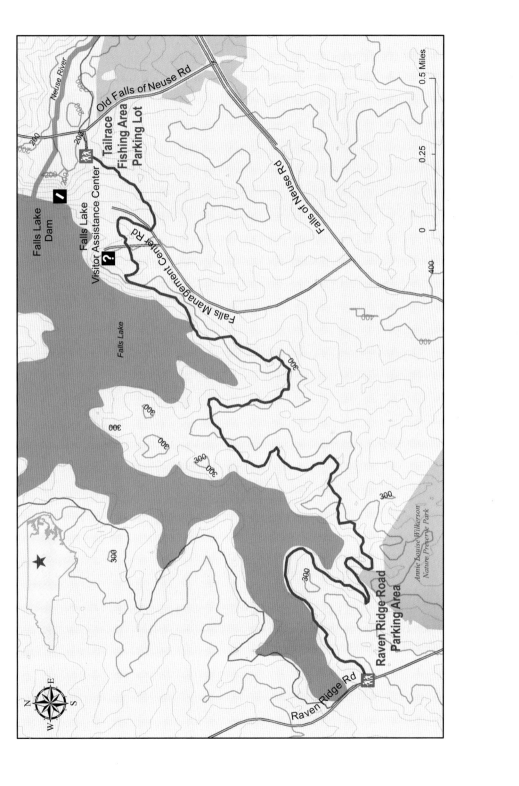

Falls Lake Dam

Falls Lake

Neuse River

Old Falls of Neuse Rd

Tailrace
Fishing Area
Parking Lot

Falls Lake
Visitor Assistance Center

Falls of Neuse Rd

Falls Management Center Rd

Falls Lake

300

300
300

300

300
300

300

300

300

Raven Ridge Road
Parking Area

Raven Ridge Rd

Annie Louise Wilkerson
Nature Preserve Park

200

200

200

0.5 Miles

0.25

0

400

400

400

N
E
S
W

300

HIKE OVERVIEW

This hike includes the easternmost portion of the Falls Lake Trail that follows nearly the entire southern shore of Falls Lake. Only coming close to roads and houses a few times along its length, the hike offers unusual solitude for its location in the suburbs of Raleigh.

Because of its fall-line geology, it also offers a surprising amount of elevation change for the Piedmont, with a third-of-a-mile descent dropping more than 100 feet to the dam trailhead. The remainder of the trail is more characteristic of the rest of the area, dipping in and out of coves and spending quality time along the lake.

The geology of the Falls Lake Trail has been extensively documented. (See "For More Information" for a link to a geologic guide to the area.) This trail section is noted for its large rock exposures of *Falls leucogneiss*, an unusual rock unit that has geological and historical significance for this part of North Carolina, as well as for abundant geological evidence of an ancient fault zone.

The hike begins just south of the Raven Ridge Rd. bridge over the lake, at a gravel pullout where the trail enters the woods by a signboard. It soon reaches the lake shore and provides intermittent views of the lake for the rest of the hike.

At mile 0.7, a connecting trail on the right leads to Annie Louise Wilkerson Nature Preserve Park, a Raleigh city park previously owned by and named for a well-known Raleigh physician. Restrooms, water, and parking are available 0.4 mile away at the park.

At mile 2.5, a blue-blazed trail on the right goes 0.6 mile to bypass the Falls Lake Visitor Assistance Center before rejoining the MST at mile 3.3. Following this trail can shave a bit off the hiking distance. At mile 2.8, the trail goes up some stairs, then crosses the exit road from the Visitor Assistance Center, which has restrooms and water. However, it is shorter and easier to access the buildings from the next road crossing at mile 2.9.

After crossing one more paved road—which leads to the crest of the Falls Lake dam on the left—the trail begins a moderately steep descent to the base of the dam and the end of the hike.

DRIVING DIRECTIONS

From I-540 in northeast Raleigh, take exit 14, Falls of Neuse Rd. At the top of the ramp, turn left onto Falls of Neuse Rd. (Because of the configuration of the exit, this is a left turn coming from either direction.)

To reach Trailhead 1, travel about 1.6 miles on Falls of Neuse Rd., then turn left on Raven Ridge Rd., the first traffic light after WakeMed North hospital. The trailhead is 1.1 miles ahead; it is just before the road crosses Falls Lake and has gravel pullouts on both sides of the road.

To reach Trailhead 2, continue straight through Raven Ridge Rd. on Falls of Neuse Rd. After another 1.9 miles, just before the road crosses the Neuse River, turn left at the sign for the Falls Tailrace Fishing Area. The parking lot is just ahead on the right.

HIKE DIRECTIONS

0.0 From the gravel pull-off just south of the Raven Ridge Rd. bridge over Falls Lake, enter the woods by a trail signboard.

0.4 Pass near the lake, then head right and then left up a cove to parallel a creek. Turn left to cross the creek on a high footbridge. On the other side of the creek, head left on a gentle ascent.

0.7 Pass a junction with a trail to Annie Louise Wilkerson Nature Preserve Park, a Raleigh city park, on the right.

0.8 Cross two footbridges over a small creek.

1.4 Cross another small creek on a footbridge. The trail ascends slightly.

1.9 Walk across a wide utility easement.

2.2 Turn right onto an open footpath, then quickly left off it. Turn right and cross a small plank walkway over a feeder creek.

2.5 Stay left at a junction with a blue-blazed trail on the right, then cross a paved service road by the lake. *Note:* The other trail goes 0.6 mile to bypass the Falls Lake Visitor Assistance Center before it rejoins the MST.

2.8 Climb a set of stairs, then turn right to follow a paved path for about 100 yards. Go left to cross a paved road, the exit from the Visitor Assistance Center, and enter an area of young-growth pine.

2.9 Cross another section of the paved access road as the trail reenters a short patch of woods. *Note:* Restrooms and water are within view to your left.

3.1 Cross a short boardwalk, then emerge from the woods to follow a wide gravel path past a wildlife-viewing blind (pay attention to trail markings through this section). Turn right, then left, to cross the Falls Lake dam access road (the dam is left) and reenter the woods.

3.3 Pass a junction with a blue-blazed trail (mentioned at mile 2.5) on the right.

3.4 By some trail signage, turn right onto a gravel access road.

3.5 Reach the parking lot of the Tailrace Fishing Area, just below the dam, and the end of this hike.

SPECIAL CONSIDERATIONS

Hunting is allowed on game lands in Durham and Wake Counties by Falls Lake, including much of this hike (archery only). When you are on the trail around Falls Lake, assume you are on game lands unless the book or signs state otherwise. Hunting is prohibited on Sunday. You can find more information about hunting seasons and the Butner–Falls of Neuse Game Land at www.ncwildlife.org/Hunting.

FOR MORE INFORMATION

Falls Lake Map: files.nc.gov/ncparks/maps-and-brochures/falls-lake -state-recreation-area-map.pdf

Butner-Falls of Neuse Game Land Map: www.ncwildlife.org/Portals/0 /Hunting/Game-Land-Maps/Piedmont/Butner-Falls-of-Neuse.pdf

To purchase a beautifully detailed map of the Falls Lake Trail from Old Oxford Hwy. near Penny's Bend on the Eno River to Falls Lake dam: artshikingmaps.info

US Army Corps of Engineers at Falls Lake: www.saw.usace.army.mil /Locations/DistrictLakesandDams/FallsLake.aspx

Falls Lake State Recreation Area: www.ncparks.gov/falls-lake-state -recreation-area

Geologic guide for Falls Lake: www.ncgeology.com/falls_lake_geology /pages/TrailGuide_FallsLake_home.html

Annie Louise Wilkerson Nature Preserve Park: www.raleighnc.gov/parks /content/ParksRec/Articles/Parks/AnnieWilkerson.html

Coastal Plain and
Outer Banks Region

Hike 24

RALEIGH'S NEUSE RIVER GREENWAY

Buffaloe Road to Milburnie Park

Pedestrian suspension bridge over the Neuse River. Photo by Betsy Brown.

Distance: 4.4 miles one-way (4.1 miles on MST plus 0.3-mile spur to parking); 8.8 miles round-trip
Degree of difficulty: Easy
Trail type: Paved greenway
Trailhead 1: Buffaloe Rd. boat access (4901 Elizabeth Dr.); no facilities
Trailhead 1 coordinates: N35.84771, W78.53089
Trailhead 1 elevation: 190 feet
Trailhead 2: Milburnie Park at Allen Dr.; no facilities
Trailhead 2 coordinates: N35.80127, W78.54112
Trailhead 2 elevation: 220 feet
Total elevation change: gain, 211 feet; loss, 181 feet
MST segment: 11
Highlights: Elegant river bridge; good river views; rapids at historic dam site
Dogs: Allowed on leash

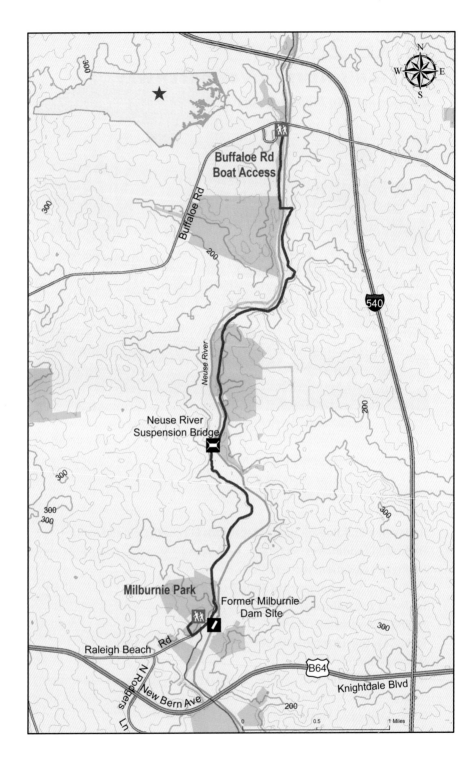

HIKE OVERVIEW

Raleigh's Neuse River Trail stretches almost 28 miles from Falls Lake dam to the Johnston County line, where it changes name and continues on into the town of Clayton. The paved greenway, as the name suggests, parallels the Neuse River for most of its length. It runs concurrently with the MST for its entire length. This hike includes one of the most scenic portions of the greenway.

Near the end of the hike is the former site of the Milburnie Dam. This 15-foot-high dam, most recently built in 1900 (previous dams dated back to the late 1700s), was the last remaining impoundment on the Neuse below Falls Lake. The dam was removed in 2017, allowing the Neuse to run unimpeded over 200 miles from Falls Lake to the Pamlico Sound.

Before its removal, the Milburnie Dam created a 6.6-mile-long lake that stretched the entire length of this hike. Thus, hikers on this stretch have an opportunity to watch the progress of the river environment returning to its natural state: mudflats transforming into meadows, wetlands, and forests; native fish returning to their historic spawning grounds upstream; and riffles and rapids forming as the river channel returns to its original bed.

The hike begins just downstream of the Buffaloe Rd. bridge over the Neuse, at the Buffaloe Rd. boat access. A short spur leads to the MST proper, where hikers will turn right to continue downstream. At mile 0.5, a trail on the right leads to Buffaloe Rd. Athletic Park, which features numerous ball fields, an aquatic center, a track, and a playground, along with restrooms and drinking water. Just beyond, the trail crosses the Neuse River for the first time.

Over the next 2.0 miles, the trail continues through woods close to the riverside, crossing several smaller creeks and wetlands, before crossing the Neuse again on the Skycrest Suspension Bridge. At 275 feet, this is the longest pedestrian suspension bridge in North Carolina (tied with the greenway's other suspension bridge upstream at Horseshoe Farm Park).

Shortly after the crossing, another trail on the right leads to Abington Ln. A parking lot here provides an opportunity to shorten the hike.

Another trail on the right at mile 3.6 leads to Crag Burn Ln., but no parking is available at this location. Soon after the side path, the greenway passes an interpretive sign describing the wetland the path crosses here.

At mile 4.1, after another interpretive sign, is the former Milburnie Dam site. Just below here, this hike turns right from the MST onto a spur trail to the road and parking area. Almost 0.1 mile farther on the MST, however, is another bridge over the Neuse that provides good views back over the Milburnie Dam site.

DRIVING DIRECTIONS

To reach Trailhead 1, the Buffaloe Rd. boat access, from I-440, Raleigh's Beltway, take exit 11 onto Capital Blvd. (US 1/401 North) toward Wake Forest and Louisburg. Continue approximately 1.9 miles, then turn right on Buffaloe Rd. After 3.5 miles, just before crossing the Neuse River, turn right on Elizabeth Dr. Go 0.2 mile to the end of the road and turn right into the parking area.

To reach Trailhead 2, Milburnie Park, from I-440, take exit 13B onto US 64 East toward Knightdale. After 1.9 miles, turn left on Rogers Ln. Continue 0.3 mile, then turn right on Raleigh Beach Rd. Follow this 0.3 mile until it makes a sharp left and becomes Allen Dr. The parking lot and trailhead are at the end of the road.

HIKE DIRECTIONS

0.0 From the parking lot, walk 100 feet to a T-intersection and turn right on the Neuse River Trail / MST.

0.2 Cross bridge #234; there are houses on the right.

0.5 Cross bridge #235, then continue past a trail on the right leading to Buffaloe Rd. Athletic Park.

0.6 Cross the Neuse River on a long bridge (#237–239).

1.1 Cross bridge #240.

1.4 Cross bridge #241.

2.2 Cross bridge #242.

2.6 Cross the Neuse River on the Skycrest Suspension Bridge (#243–245).

2.7 Pass a trail leading to Abington Ln. on the right.

2.8 Cross bridges #246 and #247.

3.6 Pass a trail leading to Crag Burn Ln. on the right.

3.7 Pass an interpretive sign, "A Wetland's Work Is Never Done." In a few yards, cross bridge #98, an old bridge with great views of the wetland around the Neuse River.

3.9 Continue straight past a trail leading to Allen Dr. and Milburnie Park.

4.0 Pass an interpretive sign, "River Crossing," on the left.

4.1   Pass the former Milburnie Dam site on the left, then turn right from the MST onto the trail heading to Raleigh Beach Rd.

4.2   Reach a road intersection and turn right onto Allen Dr.

4.4   Continue into Allen Dr. parking lot and the end of the hike.

FOR MORE INFORMATION

Raleigh MST / Neuse River Trail (scroll to middle of page for link to pdf): www.raleighnc.gov/parks/content/ParksRec/Articles/Greenways /NeuseRiverTrail.html

Hike 25
SMITHFIELD'S NEUSE RIVERWALK
Smithfield Recreation and Aquatics Center to
Bob Wallace Jaycee Kiddie Park

Smithfield's Neuse Riverwalk. Photo by Chris Johnson.

Distance: 3.1 miles one-way; 6.2 miles round-trip
Degree of difficulty: Easy
Trail type: Paved greenway
Trailhead 1: Smithfield Recreation and Aquatics Center; water, restrooms
Trailhead 1 coordinates: N35.53001, W78.33021
Trailhead 1 elevation: 141 feet
Trailhead 2: Bob Wallace Jaycee Kiddie Park; no facilities
Trailhead 2 coordinates: N35.50920, W78.34932
Trailhead 2 elevation: 129 feet
Total elevation change: gain, 73 feet; loss, 85 feet
MST segment: 11
Highlights: River views; quaint trail town
Dogs: Allowed on leash

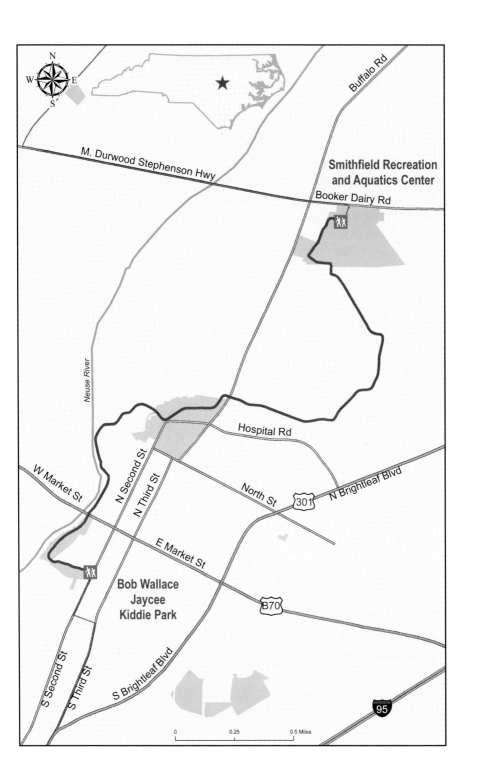

HIKE OVERVIEW

This hike offers a pleasant riverside amble along a paved greenway into the heart of Smithfield. It begins from the west side of the parking lot on a white sidewalk, which meanders 0.4 mile along the perimeter of the park. Note the sculptures of child athletes, the educational panels along the walk, and the exercise stations with signs.

At mile 0.3, just before the sidewalk returns to the baseball fields, the MST turns right onto the asphalt Buffalo Creek Greenway (also known as Smithfield Neuse Riverwalk) at a signpost with a map. This 10-foot-wide, 2.8-mile asphalt greenway accommodates hikers, runners, and cyclists and has mileposts about every 0.2 mile. It features several educational displays and historical plaques.

At mile 2.6 (greenway milepost 0.6) are two educational displays and a boat ramp (the start of the MST's Neuse River Paddle Route). The stairs just behind the "After the Storm" display provide access to parking on Front St. and downtown Smithfield. Among the attractions here is the Ava Gardner Museum, celebrating Smithfield's most famous native.

After another 0.2 mile, the greenway passes under W. Market St. Just before the road bridge is an old stone bridge piling with a plaque at a boardwalk bridge. The covered bridge that used to stand here was built after the Civil War and used until 1907. Just after the crossing, on the left, are Legion Hut, home of the Neuse Little Theatre, and the Neuse River Amphitheatre. An asphalt path to the left leads to Front St., another way to reach downtown Smithfield.

About 0.2 mile later, the greenway turns away from the Neuse River. After passing a church cemetery on the left and another educational display, the greenway, and this hike, end at a Girl Scout Hut at Bob Wallace Jaycee Kiddie Park.

DRIVING DIRECTIONS

To reach Trailhead 1, the Smithfield Recreation and Aquatics Center, from downtown Smithfield, head north on N. Third St. to its end. Turn right on North St. and then almost immediately left on Buffalo Rd. Continue 1.2 miles to the intersection with M. Durwood Stephenson Hwy. on the left and Booker Dairy Rd. on the right. Turn right, proceed 300 yards, and make another right into the Recreation and Aquatics Center entrance.

To reach Trailhead 2, Bob Wallace Jaycee Kiddie Park, from downtown

Smithfield, head west on Market St. and turn left on S. Second St. After two blocks (just after crossing Church St.), the entrance is on the right.

HIKE DIRECTIONS

0.0 From the parking lot, begin walking to the west (the right as seen from the recreation center entrance) on the white sidewalk.

0.3 Just before returning to the baseball fields, turn right on the asphalt Buffalo Creek Greenway.

1.6 Cross under Buffalo Rd.

1.7 Cross a bridge over Buffalo Creek.

2.0 After milepost 1.4, reach an additional trailhead entrance to Buffalo Creek Greenway at N. Second St. and Hospital Rd. Bear right to stay on the greenway.

2.6 Near milepost 0.6, pass the "Where Does the Water Go" and "After the Storm" educational displays and a boat ramp.

2.7 Cross under W. Market St.

3.1 Reach the south end of the Buffalo Creek Greenway, at Bob Wallace Jaycee Kiddie Park, and the end of the hike.

FOR MORE INFORMATION

Johnston County Heritage Center: www.johnstonnc.com/heritage2 /index.cfm?CFID=31004939&CFTOKEN=45552114

Ava Gardner Museum: www.avagardner.org

Hike 26

BENTONVILLE BATTLEFIELD

Harper House to Cole Plantation

Twelve-pound Napoleon cannon at Bentonville Battlefield.
Photo by North Carolina Division of Parks and Recreation.

Distance: 2.3 miles one-way; 4.6 miles round-trip
Degree of difficulty: Easy
Trail type: Natural-surface trail
Trailhead 1: Bentonville Battlefield Visitor Center and Harper House; water, restrooms
Trailhead 1 coordinates: N35.30220, W78.32183
Trailhead 1 elevation: 184 feet
Trailhead 2: Cole Plantation Loop Walking Trail parking lot; no facilities
Trailhead 2 coordinates: N35.31628, W78.30231
Trailhead 2 elevation: 190 feet
Total elevation change: gain, 82 feet; loss, 75 feet
MST segment: 12
Highlights: Civil War battlefield with historic markers; verdant farm fields
Dogs: Allowed on leash

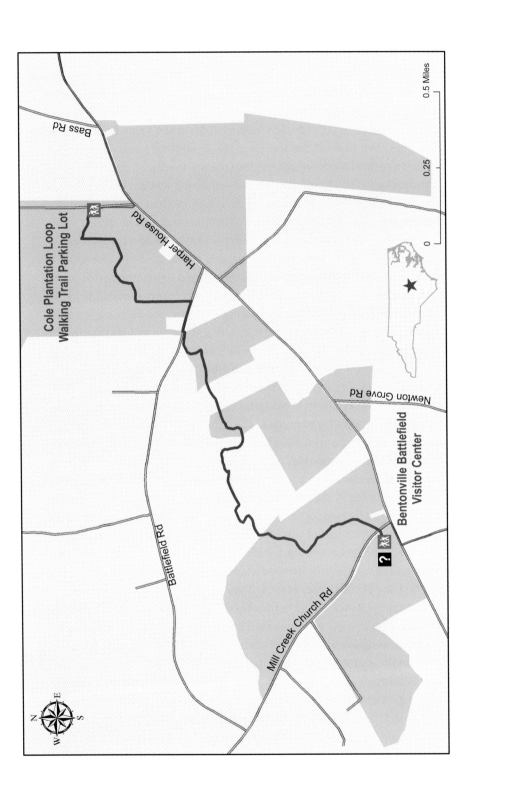

Cole Plantation Loop
Walking Trail Parking Lot

Bass Rd

Harper House Rd

Battlefield Rd

Mill Creek Church Rd

Newton Grove Rd

Bentonville Battlefield
Visitor Center

0   0.25   0.5 Miles

N
W   E
S

HIKE OVERVIEW

Bentonville Battlefield is the site of North Carolina's largest Civil War battle, fought on March 19–21, 1865. The Battle of Bentonville was the last significant attempt to stop Gen. William T. Sherman's march through the Carolinas, and marked the last time the Confederate army was able to mount a tactical offensive against the Union. The ensuing defeat considerably weakened the Confederacy's last remaining armies. The Bentonville Battlefield State Historic Site now includes more than 2,000 acres of the battlefield. It was declared a National Historic Landmark in 1996.

This hike follows a recently opened trail that meanders through woods and fields, along the 1865 battle lines, and across surviving remnants of earthworks built for the battle. It is well marked with interpretive panels and plaques and historical displays that help hikers envision how the battle unfolded. Along with this walking-only trail, the Bentonville Battlefield Driving Tour, some of which is included in the current MST route, provides additional insights into the battle's events.

The hike and surrounding areas also provide a glimpse into why Friends of the MST calls Segment 12 of the MST the "Agricultural Heartland." Johnston County ranks fourth in North Carolina in crop production and eighth in agriculture overall, and much of the agricultural land is concentrated in the south of the county, where this hike is located. Neighboring Sampson County, which encompasses most of Segment 12, is ranked first in crops, second in livestock and poultry, and first overall. Agricultural products people might see in the area include tobacco, cotton, hogs, turkeys, cattle, soybeans, and timber. Some of these products are usually visible along the trail in the second half of this hike, which skirts several agricultural fields.

The hike begins at the Bentonville Battlefield Visitor Center, which features an audiovisual program and a large fiber-optic map exhibit depicting the first day of the battle, as well as several other maps and exhibits. The neighboring Harper House is furnished as a Civil War field hospital. The visitor center and Harper House are open 9:00 A.M.–5:00 P.M., Tuesday–Saturday, and have water, restrooms, and a drink machine.

From the visitor center, the route crosses Mill Creek Church Rd. and continues through an open field to a gap in earthworks, next to a cannon, where it enters the woods and begins the self-guided historic trail. For the first mile, the route goes back and forth between woods and fields, finally coming out and staying mostly along the edges of agricultural fields for the last 1.2 miles. The hike ends at the Cole Plantation Loop Walking Trail parking lot, where another 1.5-mile loop trail, not part of the MST, explores additional parts of the battlefield.

DRIVING DIRECTIONS

From I-40, take exit 341 and turn west on NC 50. After about a quarter mile, take the first right, at the flashing light, to stay on NC 50. Continue 1.6 miles, then turn right on Harper House Rd. After 5.0 more miles, the Bentonville Battlefield Visitor Center, Trailhead 1, is on the left. Turn left on Mill Creek Church Rd., then immediately left into the parking lot.

To reach Trailhead 2, the Cole Plantation Loop Walking Trail parking lot, return to Harper House Rd. and turn left. Drive 1.4 miles, then turn left on the gravel road signed to the parking lot, which is about 200 feet ahead.

HIKE DIRECTIONS

0.0 Walk out the Bentonville Battlefield Visitor Center and Harper House driveway, then cross Mill Creek Church Rd. Walk across the field toward an informational panel on the left side.

0.1 Pass through a gap in the remains of earthworks near a cannon and enter the woods.

0.4 Cross a bridge over old earthworks, then pass between a bench and informational plaque near a road. Bear right back into the woods.

0.5 Turn right at a T-intersection, then cross a set of earthworks.

0.6 Emerge to a field and turn left, following signs around the left side of the field.

0.8 At the end of the field, turn left at the arrow onto a path leading into the woods.

0.9 Pass the remains of trenches and a bench on the left.

1.0 Cross a boardwalk bridge over two small streams.

1.1 Reach a field and continue straight along the left side.

1.2 Pass through a line of trees and continue along the edge of the next field.

1.4 Turn sharply left to continue walking on the edge of the field.

1.5 Cross Battlefield Rd. at the crosswalk and turn right to walk along the road.

1.6 Just before a barn with a silo, turn left on a sandy track running through a field.

1.8 At the end of the track, turn right and walk along the edge of the field, then continue onto a grassy path next to a small pond. After emerging to the next field, turn left to stay on its edge.

2.0 Turn left to cross a gas pipeline easement in a swale, then continue straight across the field.

2.2 At the end of the field, in front of a small graveyard, turn right and continue along the edge of the field.

2.3 Reach the Cole Plantation Loop Walking Trail parking lot, the end of the hike.

SPECIAL CONSIDERATIONS

Much of the hike is on private land. Please stay on the trail and do not enter the fields unless the trail specifically goes through them.

FOR MORE INFORMATION

Bentonville Battlefield: historicsites.nc.gov/bentonville-battlefield

Bentonville Battlefield Driving Tour Map: files.nc.gov/dncr-historicsites /brentonville-battlefield_tour_map.pdf (Note the spelling "brentonville" is in the URL itself.)

Hike 27
DOWNTOWN ROSEBORO LOOP

Downtown Roseboro and town park. Photo by Ben Jones.

Distance: 1.9-mile loop (1.2 on MST, 0.7 on other roads)
Degree of difficulty: Easy
Trail type: Paved road
Trailhead: Shopping center at NC 24 and Culbreth St.; food, water, supplies, restrooms
Trailhead coordinates: N34.95842, W78.51415
Trailhead elevation: 127 feet
Total elevation change: gain, 12 feet; loss, 12 feet
MST segment: 12
Highlights: Quaint and historic trail town
Dogs: Allowed on leash

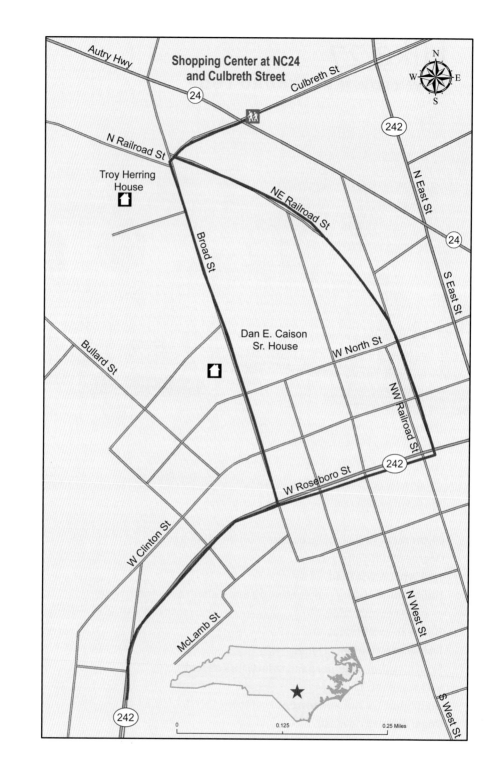

Shopping Center at NC24
and Culbreth Street

Autry Hwy

24

Culbreth St

242

N Railroad St

N East St

Troy Herring
House

NE Railroad St

24

Broad St

S East St

Dan E. Caison
Sr. House

W North St

Bullard St

NW Railroad St

242

W Roseboro St

W Clinton St

McLamb St

N West St

242

0   0.125   0.25 Miles

S West St

HIKE OVERVIEW

Roseboro, a town of about 1,200 residents, came into being around 1890 as a depot along the Cape Fear & Yadkin Valley Railroad line, which ran from Fayetteville to Wilmington. It boasted the first drugstore and bank in Sampson County, along with its first auto dealership. This hike highlights both the town's history and its present.

From the trailhead at the shopping center, the route crosses NC 24 (Dr. Martin Luther King Jr. Blvd.) on Culbreth St. After one block, it takes the sharp left onto N. East Railroad St., paralleling the grade of the old Cape Fear & Yadkin Valley Railroad bed into downtown Roseboro.

At mile 0.4, the route passes the remains of an old brick cone silo, used to burn off scrap lumber that was too small for the local mill. The trail continues alongside a town park built on the former railroad grade, passing a community garden on the right. (Plans are to eventually shift the MST to the railroad bed.) At the end of the park, near the historic railroad depot, it turns onto Roseboro St., the heart of downtown.

Leaving downtown, the hike passes through a leafy residential area. The end of the sidewalk marks the far end of the loop. The route returns along Roseboro St. and turns left on Broad St., just beyond the Butler Funeral Home.

Although not part of the MST, the return route offers a shorter, direct route back to the beginning that also passes two homes on the National Register of Historic Places. The first, the Dan E. Caison Sr. House, is on the left at mile 1.6, between North and McPherson Sts. It was built in 1924 and is considered one of the finest examples of an American Craftsman–style bungalow in Sampson County. The second is the Troy Herring House, on the left at mile 1.8, just before the intersection with Culbreth St. This large, two-story house, dating from 1912, was built for the owner of the local lumber mill and is the most elaborate of the county's Classical Revival houses.

After passing the Troy Herring House, the route turns right on Culbreth St., crosses NC 24, and returns to the trailhead at the shopping center.

DRIVING DIRECTIONS

From I-95, take exit 52A onto NC 24 East toward Clinton. Continue approximately 17 miles into Roseboro.

From I-40, take exit 364 onto NC 24 West and follow NC 24 signs through Clinton. From Clinton, it is roughly another 11 miles on NC 24 to Roseboro.

Coming from either direction, take the business route of NC 24 into Roseboro. Parking for the trailhead is at a shopping center off NC 24 between its intersections with Broad St. and Culbreth St.

HIKE DIRECTIONS

0.0 Leave the shopping center parking lot on Culbert St. and cross NC 24.

0.1 At a stop sign where several roads come together, take a sharp left onto N. East Railroad St.

0.4 Pass the remains of an old kiln on the right. At a stop sign in front of the Temple of God and Roseboro Masons Lodge, bear right to stay on N. East Railroad St.

0.5 Cross E. Clinton St., staying on the left side of the divided road (going against one-way traffic).

0.6 At a T-intersection in front of the historic Roseboro train depot and town park, turn right on W. Roseboro St.

0.7 Pass the Roseboro public library on the right.

0.8 Continue through the intersection with Broad St.

1.0 Bear left as Owens Ave. joins from the right.

1.1 Reach the end of the sidewalk and return to Broad St.

1.4 Turn left on Broad St., leaving the MST.

1.6 Pass the Dan E. Caison Sr. House on the left.

1.8 Pass the Troy Herring House on the left, then turn right on Culbreth St.

1.9 Cross NC 24 and return to the shopping center parking lot.

SPECIAL CONSIDERATIONS

As the route is entirely on city streets, hikers should use caution and stay on sidewalks wherever possible.

FOR MORE INFORMATION

Town of Roseboro: www.roseboronc.com

Sampson County Convention and Visitors Bureau: www.visitsampsonnc
.com

Hike 28

OLD CAPE FEAR COUNTRYSIDE

White Oak Post Office to Harmony Hall

Harmony Hall General Store.
Photo by Beerdra.

Distance: 2.1 miles one-way; 4.2 miles round-trip
Degree of difficulty: Easy
Trail type: Paved road
Trailhead 1: White Oak Post Office; no facilities
Trailhead 1 coordinates: N34.75108, W78.70729
Trailhead 1 elevation: 59 feet
Trailhead 2: Harmony Hall Plantation Historic Site; no facilities
Trailhead 2 coordinates: N34.74066, W78.73825
Trailhead 2 elevation: 72 feet
Total elevation change: gain, 21 feet; loss, 8 feet
MST segment: 13
Highlights: Revolutionary War historic plantation; rural community and
     countryside
Dogs: Allowed on leash

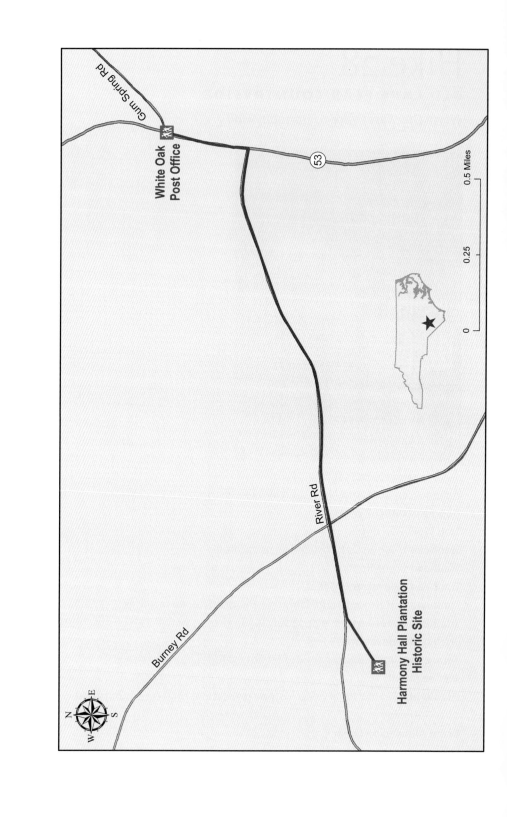

White Oak
Post Office

Gum Spring Rd

53

River Rd

Burney Rd

Harmony Hall Plantation
Historic Site

N
W E
S

0   0.25   0.5 Miles

HIKE OVERVIEW

The primary highlight of this short hike is Harmony Hall Plantation Historic Site, which was added to the National Register of Historic Places in 1972. Located approximately a mile from the Cape Fear River—out of flood danger—Harmony Hall features one of the oldest surviving residences in North Carolina, built in the 1760s by Col. James Richardson. Richardson was a sea trader and won recognition as a British soldier during the French and Indian War. He was an officer in the colonial militia during the American Revolution and went on to become a representative in the North Carolina General Assembly. He died in 1810.

Local lore says that during the Revolution, while Col. Richardson was away fighting in South Carolina, Cornwallis lodged at Harmony Hall. During Cornwallis's evening meetings with his officers, Richardson's wife crept up to the attic and overheard their conversations. She dispatched a letter to her husband warning him of Cornwallis's plans to march on Wilmington. This information supposedly played a part in his ultimate defeat at Yorktown. No historical evidence exists to confirm this legend.

The Harmony Hall plantation house and grounds, including some outbuildings, have been restored and are maintained by a nonprofit group of volunteers who put on a variety of events throughout the year. The house is open Sundays, 2:00–4:00 P.M., or by appointment.

The hike begins at the White Oak post office and heads south on the shoulder of NC 53 through the rural community of White Oak. After passing Kaid's Grocery and Cain's Grill, friendly establishments run by avid supporters of the MST, it turns right onto River Rd., a quiet back road.

The route continues through mixed coastal-plain forests and orderly pine plantations for about 1.6 miles before reaching the entrance to Harmony Hall Plantation. A short walk down the unpaved driveway, past a quaint old general store and several plantation buildings, leads to the main plantation house and the end of the hike.

DRIVING DIRECTIONS

From I-95, take exit 31 toward St. Pauls and continue east on NC 20 for 9.8 miles. At the T-intersection, turn right onto NC 87, a divided highway. After 4.6 miles, at the main intersection in the town of Tar Heel, turn left onto Tar Heel Ferry Rd. (signed for Harmony Hall). Continue 1.7 miles, crossing the Cape Fear River, and take the next right on River Rd., again signed for

Harmony Hall. The entrance to the plantation and Trailhead 2 is 3.0 miles ahead on the right.

To reach Trailhead 1, continue on River Rd., following the hike route, for 1.6 miles, then turn left on NC 53. The post office is 0.3 mile ahead on the right.

HIKE DIRECTIONS

0.0 From the White Oak post office, head south on NC 53.

0.2 Pass Kaid's Grocery and Cain's Grill.

0.3 Turn right on River Rd. (SR 1318).

1.6 Continue straight on River Rd. through flashing yellow lights at Burney Rd.

1.9 Turn left into the Harmony Hall Plantation Historic Site.

2.1 Reach the end of the hike at the historic home at the end of the lane.

FOR MORE INFORMATION

Harmony Hall Plantation: harmonyhallplantationvillage.com
ncvisitorcenter.com/Harmony_Hall.html

Hike 29

TURNBULL CREEK AND JONES LAKE

Turnbull Creek Educational State Forest Office to

Jones Lake State Park Visitor Center

Turnbull Creek Educational State Forest turpentine still exhibit. Photo by Ben Jones.

Distance: 1.0 mile one-way (with optional 4.0-mile loop); 2.0 miles
round-trip

Degree of difficulty: Easy

Trail type: Natural-surface trail

Trailhead 1: Turnbull Creek Educational State Forest Office; no facilities

Trailhead 1 coordinates: N34.68906, W78.59018

Trailhead 1 elevation: 72 feet

Trailhead 2: Jones Lake State Park Visitor Center; restrooms, water,
snacks, picnic tables

Trailhead 2 coordinates: N34.68287, W78.59553

Trailhead 2 elevation: 69 feet

Total elevation change: gain, 17 feet; loss, 13 feet

MST segment: 13

Highlights: Carolina bay lake; longleaf pine savanna; pocosins;
educational exhibits about history and ecology of the area

Dogs: Allowed on leash

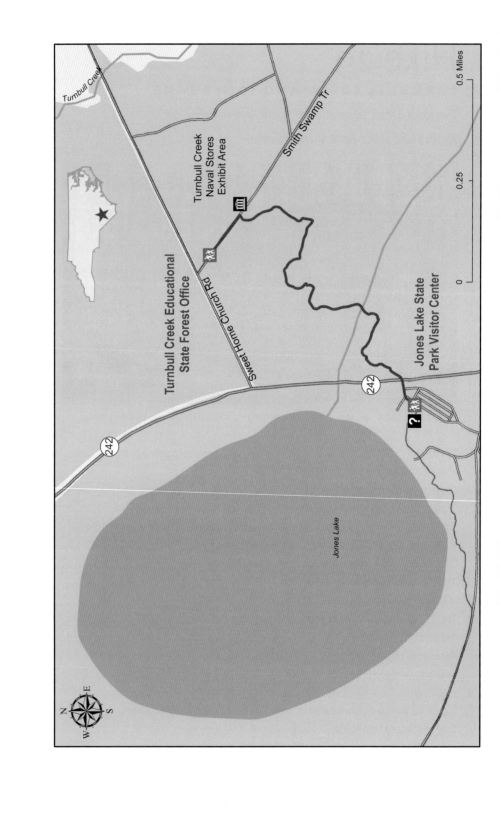

Turnbull Creek
Naval Stores
Exhibit Area

Turnbull Creek Educational
State Forest Office

Sweet Home Church Rd

Smith Swamp Tr

242

Jones Lake State
Park Visitor Center

?

Jones Lake

Turnbull Creek

242

0   0.25   0.5 Miles

N
W   E
S

HIKE OVERVIEW

Carolina bays, named for the evergreen bay trees that thrive in many of them, are elliptical depressions, all aligned in a northwest–southeast direction. The bays occur all over southeastern North Carolina and provide habitat for many rare and endangered species. Although theories abound about how they were originally formed, nobody really knows. This hike features two of these bays—one that still holds water and one that has dried and filled with vegetation.

Beginning at the Turnbull Creek Educational State Forest office, the hike goes on Smith Swamp Trail, a sandy road, through upland, longleaf pine forest, home to several red-cockaded woodpecker nests. After about 0.2 mile, it turns right onto another, less well-maintained, sandy road. On Smith Swamp Trail, just beyond this turnoff, is an educational area featuring information about historic longleaf pine harvesting and treatment practices for the naval stores industry.

The road descends into a pocosin ecosystem, the remains of a former Carolina bay. Here, the forest is a little wetter and has mostly hardwoods, especially holly, bay, oaks, and maples.

The trail crosses the Jones Lake drain on a bridge, then follows the drain through a picturesque area for a short distance before rising back up to longleaf pine forest.

The hike crosses NC 242 at the entrance to Jones Lake State Park and ends at the park's visitor center. The visitor center is open 8:00 A.M.–5:00 P.M. weekdays (closed on state holidays), and features water, restrooms, refreshments, and educational exhibits. The pier behind it provides fine views of the lake, an example of a Carolina bay still holding water.

For hikers seeking a longer walk, the park's Bay Trail forms a 4-mile loop around the lake. The first 1.4 miles (going clockwise) are part of the MST.

DRIVING DIRECTIONS

From I-95 near Lumberton, take exit 20, turning toward Lumberton on Roberts St. at the top of the exit ramp. Continue on Roberts St. for 1.6 miles, then turn left on Elizabethtown Rd. (NC 41), signed to Elizabethtown. After 16.9 miles, NC 87 joins from the left; 1.7 miles later, turn left onto NC 41 East / Business NC 87, signed to Elizabethtown and White Lake. Continue 4.4 miles, into downtown Elizabethtown, then turn left on NC 41 East / US 701, signed to Jones Lake State Park. After 1.3 miles, turn left on NC 53

West / NC 242 North, signed to Jones Lake State Park and Bladen Lakes State Forest. Almost immediately, turn right to stay on NC 242. The entrance to Jones Lake State Park is 2.7 miles ahead on the left.

To reach the trailhead at Turnbull Creek State Educational Forest, continue 0.3 mile on NC 242, then turn right on Sweet Home Church Rd. at the sign to the educational forest. The entrance is 0.3 mile ahead on the right.

HIKE DIRECTIONS

0.0 Begin the hike at the Turnbull Creek Experimental State Forest office. From the parking area, turn left onto Smith Swamp Trail.

0.1 Turn right on a loose, sandy road just before a set of exhibits about the history of the naval stores industry.

0.3 Turn right on a logging road. The trail will begin to go down a bit, entering a pocosin. Stay right at the fork, then follow the trail, which goes on and off the logging road and eventually crosses the road.

0.4 Pass through a low area that may be wet after rains.

0.6 Bear left onto a logging road.

0.7 Cross a bridge over the Jones Lake drain. The trail will begin to rise up to slightly higher ground and leave the pocosin.

0.9 Cross NC 242 and continue on the Jones Lake State Park driveway.

1.0 Reach the Jones Lake State Park Visitor Center and the end of the hike.

SPECIAL CONSIDERATIONS

Mosquitos are very prevalent on this hike, especially in the summer. We recommend wearing insect repellent whenever hiking here and avoiding the hike if the weather has been wet recently.

The Jones Lake State Park is open 8:00 A.M.–6:00 P.M. November–February; 8:00 A.M.–8:00 P.M. March–May and September–October; and 8:00 A.M.–9:00 P.M. June–August. It is closed on Christmas Day. When the park is closed, the park gate is closed and locked, and it may not be possible to get a car out.

FOR MORE INFORMATION

Jones Lake State Park Map: files.nc.gov/ncparks/maps-and-brochures /jones-lake-park-map.pdf

Carolina Bays: en.wikipedia.org/wiki/Carolina_bays
Jones Lake State Park: www.ncparks.gov/jones-lake-state-park
Turnbull Creek Educational State Forest: www.ncesf.org/turnbull.html
North Carolina Birding Trail: ncbirdingtrail.org/sites/2012/8/1/jones-lake
  -state-park.html

Hike 30
MOORES CREEK NATIONAL
BATTLEFIELD LOOP

Oak tree, Moores Creek National Battlefield. Photo by Betsy Brown.

Distance: 0.9-mile loop
Degree of difficulty: Easy
Trail type: Improved trail
Trailhead: Moores Creek National Battlefield; restrooms, water, food, picnic
Trailhead coordinates: N34.45796, W78.10857
Trailhead elevation: 25 feet
Total elevation change: gain, 20 feet; loss, 20 feet
MST segment: 14
Highlights: Site of one of the most important battles of the Revolutionary War; diverse coastal-plain ecosystems; birding
Dogs: Allowed on leash

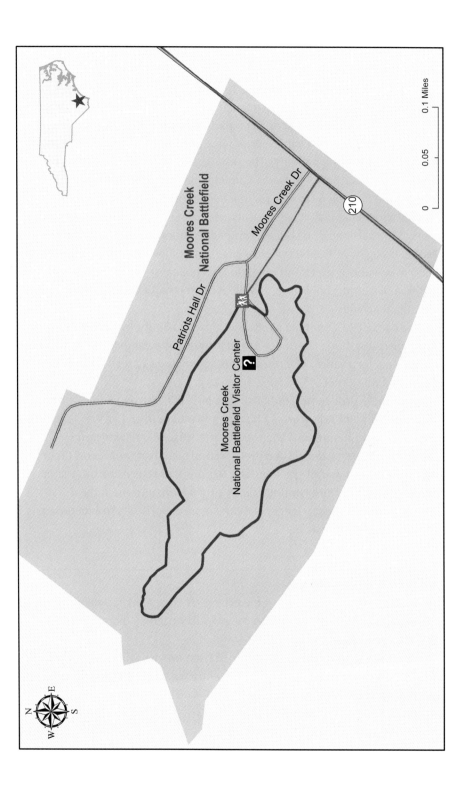

Moores Creek
National Battlefield

Patriots Hall Dr

Moores Creek Dr

210

Moores Creek
National Battlefield Visitor Center

0   0.05   0.1 Miles

HIKE OVERVIEW

Moores Creek National Battlefield is the site of the first Patriot victory in the American Revolution. Early on the morning of February 27, 1776, loyalist militia forces charged across the partially dismantled Moores Creek Bridge. Expecting only a small Patriot force, they were surprised by nearly 1,000 troops waiting patiently. The resulting Patriot victory signaled the end of British authority in North Carolina and led to North Carolina becoming the first colony to vote for independence.

This short loop walk takes visitors past some of the most important sites of the battlefield, as well as monuments to some of the heroes of the battle. It begins at the battlefield visitor center (open Tuesday–Saturday, 9:00 A.M.–5:00 P.M.; closed on all federal holidays), which features exhibits, a film, and a bookstore, as well as restrooms, water fountains, and vending machines.

The battlefield's multiple habitats in close proximity, including a longleaf pine restoration area, other upland forests, and swamp forest, make it a good spot for a variety of birds, and it is designated as a unit of the North Carolina Birding Trail.

From the visitor center, the hike goes past the restrooms to a left on Negro Head Point Rd., a grassy historic trace built in the 1700s. After a short distance, it shifts off the road to the History Trail, which forms a loop through the battlefield and over a reconstruction of the Moores Creek Bridge. Near the end of the loop, the History Trail returns to the visitor center lot, but this hike continues with a right turn onto the Tarheel Trail, which provides a slightly longer walk and more opportunity to experience the coastal-plain forest.

DRIVING DIRECTIONS

From I-40, take exit 408 and go west on NC 210. After 5.2 miles, at a T-intersection, turn left to stay on NC 210. After 0.2 mile more, turn right to once again stay on NC 210.

After another 9.0 miles, turn left to stay on NC 210, following signs to Moores Creek National Battlefield. The entrance to the battlefield is 1.4 miles ahead on the right.

HIKE DIRECTIONS

0.0 From the visitor center, return toward the entrance road, then turn left on the grassy trace just beyond the end of the parking lot and continue down the slope.

0.1 Shift to the left off Negro Head Point Rd. onto the History Trail, which is "paved" with shredded tire fragments.

0.2 Turn left onto an asphalt trail. A dirt trail to the right—Negro Head Point Rd. again—leads to the Patriots Hall pavilion and picnic area. Just ahead on the asphalt trail is the Stage Rd. monument. After a hundred yards, bear right at a fork in the trail, descending toward Moores Creek. Continue as the trail changes to a boardwalk through a cypress wetland and crosses Moores Creek, then becomes an asphalt trail again.

0.4 Bear left onto a gravel trail, then cross the 1999 reconstruction of the historic bridge over Moores Creek.

0.5 Keep right at the trail intersection and follow the "rubber road" past several impressive monuments and specimen trees.

0.7 Turn right onto the Tarheel Trail, another rubber-paved walking trail, just before reaching the visitor center parking lot.

0.9 Return to the visitor center parking lot and the end of the hike.

SPECIAL CONSIDERATIONS

The park is open 9:00 A.M.–5:00 P.M. every day, but is closed on federal holidays. When it is closed, there is no access to the trails.

FOR MORE INFORMATION

Moores Creek National Battlefield: www.nps.gov/mocr/index.htm

Moores Creek National Battlefield Map: www.nps.gov/mocr/planyour visit/maps.htm

North Carolina Birding Trail: ncbirdingtrail.org/sites/2012/8/1/moores -creek-national-battlefield.html

Hike 31
BURGAW GREENWAY LOOP

Historic Burgaw train depot. Photo by Carolyn Mejia.

Distance: 2.7-mile loop (2.0 miles on MST plus 0.7-mile connector to complete loop)
Degree of difficulty: Easy
Trail type: Paved greenway and sidewalk
Trailhead: Pender County Museum; no facilities
Trailhead coordinates: N34.55214, W77.92944
Trailhead elevation: 49 feet
Total elevation change: gain, 39 feet; loss, 39 feet
MST segment: 14
Highlights: Greenway trail through historic trail town
Dogs: Allowed on leash

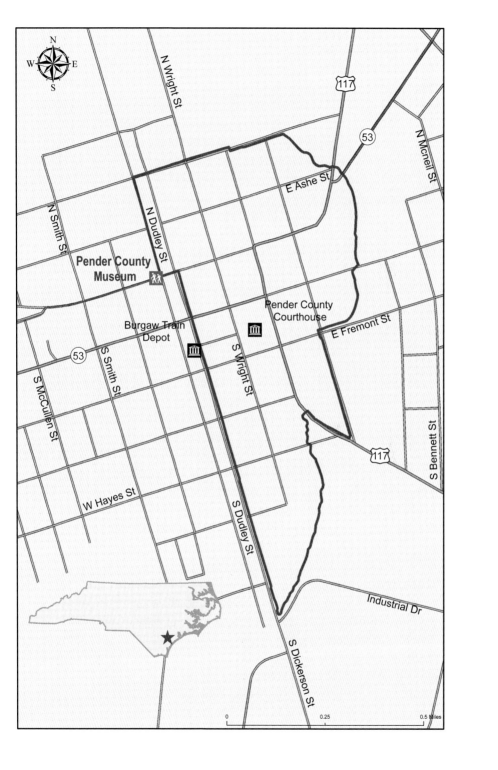

N

W ⊕ E

S

N Wright St

117

53

N Mcneil St

E Ashe St

N Smith St

N Dudley St

Pender County
Museum 🏃

Pender County
Courthouse

E Fremont St

Burgaw Train
Depot

53

🏛

S Smith St

🏛

S Wright St

S McCullen St

E Fremont St

S Bennett St

117

W Hayes St

S Dudley St

Industrial Dr

S Dickerson St

0   0.25   0.5 Miles

HIKE OVERVIEW

This easy, flat loop hike begins and ends at the Pender County Museum near downtown Burgaw. If you arrive during its operating hours (Thursday and Friday 1:00–4:00 P.M., Saturday 10:00 A.M.–2:00 P.M.), stop in to learn a little about the history of Burgaw and the surrounding area. The hike begins on Bridgers St. (facing the street from the museum, turn left), but almost immediately turns right onto the sidewalk of Dickerson St. to join the Osgood Canal Greenway and Urban Trail, a 2.7-mile loop around the Burgaw Historic District. The trail has mile markers every quarter mile and is all sidewalk or asphalt greenway.

Between miles 0.2 and 0.3, the route passes between the historic Burgaw Train Depot, the oldest in North Carolina (built circa 1850) and home to a small transportation museum, on the right and downtown Burgaw on the left. Other notable buildings in the historic district and near the trail include the Georgian Revival Pender County Courthouse, constructed in 1934; commercial buildings along W. Fremont St., mostly built in the first third of the twentieth century; and the Burgaw Presbyterian Church, constructed around 1880.

At mile 0.8, the sidewalk becomes an asphalt path, which turns sharply left to leave Dickerson St. Passing between several schools, the greenway skirts the edge of a field, then enters the woods at mile 1.0. It continues on sidewalks through a residential neighborhood before reentering a wooded area.

At mile 2.0, this hike leaves the MST, which continues northeast on NC 53. The hike continues along the Osgood Canal trail, soon returning to sidewalks. It passes Hankins Park and Burgaw Elementary School before returning to the Pender County Museum to complete the loop.

DRIVING DIRECTIONS

From I-40, take exit 398 and turn onto NC 53 toward Burgaw. After 2.0 miles, at a T-intersection, turn left to stay on NC 53, signed toward Historic Downtown Burgaw. Stay straight on this road (also known as Bridgers St.) 0.4 mile to N. Dudley St. (Do not turn left again to stay on NC 53.) The museum is on the right just past N. Dudley St.

HIKE DIRECTIONS

0.0 From the Pender County Museum, turn left on W. Bridgers St. Cross N. Dudley St., then turn right on N. Dickerson St. and walk on the sidewalk. *Note*: You are now on the Osgood Canal Greenway and Urban Trail, a 2.6-mile loop around the Burgaw Historic District.

0.2 Cross W. Wilmington St.

0.3 Continue on S. Dickerson St. in front of the Burgaw Train Depot, just before reaching W. Fremont St.

0.8 Just past Burgaw Middle School, the sidewalk changes to asphalt and takes a sharp left near Industrial Dr. Follow the asphalt path toward Rotary Park (colorful playground equipment, restrooms, and running water).

1.0 Continue on the path into the woods.

1.1 Cross Hayes St. (no street sign) into Johnson Park. Bear right onto a concrete sidewalk at a dedication plaque and a large oak tree surrounded by benches.

1.2 Go right on S. Walker St.

1.4 Turn left on S. Cowan St.

1.6 Cross E. Fremont St. and turn right to follow the sidewalk.

1.7 The sidewalk bears left, changes to asphalt, and winds through Fremont Street Park and Wilmington Street Park.

1.8 Cross E. Wilmington St., following white hash marks to jog right and then left to stay on the asphalt path.

2.0 Cross NC 53 (Jacksonville Hwy.) and N. Timberly Ln. (US 117) on white hash marks. The MST continues east on NC 53, but stay on the asphalt greenway path to complete this loop. Cars heading east on NC 53 have limited visibility, so cross with caution.

2.1 Turn left along E. Wallace St. (Look for a wastewater treatment plant sign immediately across the street.)

2.2 Follow white hash marks to cross E. Wallace St. at Hankins Park (on the left side of E. Wallace). Directly beside this street crossing in Hankins Park is a heated restroom with running water. Continue down E. Wallace.

2.3 Pass Burgaw Elementary School on E. Wallace St. and continue across N. Wright St.

2.4 Turn left on N. Dudley St.

2.7 Turn right on W. Bridgers St. and return to the Pender County Museum to complete the hike.

SPECIAL CONSIDERATIONS
Use caution crossing roads.

FOR MORE INFORMATION
Pender County Tourism: www.visitpender.com
Pender County Museum: pendercountymuseum.webs.com
Town of Burgaw: www.townofburgaw.com
Burgaw Train Depot: www.townofburgaw.com/depot
Osgood Canal Greenway Map: www.townofburgaw.com/Data/Sites/1
/media/residents/osgood-canal-trail_map-with-streets-and-legend
.pdf

Hike 32
STONES CREEK GAME LAND *NC 210 to US 17*

Stones Creek Game Land. Photo by Betsy Brown.

Distance: 3.5 miles one-way; 7.0 miles round-trip
Degree of difficulty: Moderate
Trail type: Natural-surface trail
Trailhead 1: Stones Creek Game Land entrance at NC 210; no facilities
Trailhead 1 coordinates: N34.55767, W77.44672
Trailhead 1 elevation: 66 feet
Trailhead 2: Stones Creek Game Land entrance at US 17; no facilities
Trailhead 2 coordinates: N34.56363, W77.49163
Trailhead 2 elevation: 66 feet
Total elevation change: gain, 85 feet; loss, 85 feet
MST segment: 15
Highlights: Trail through longleaf pine savanna; lake views
Dogs: Allowed on leash

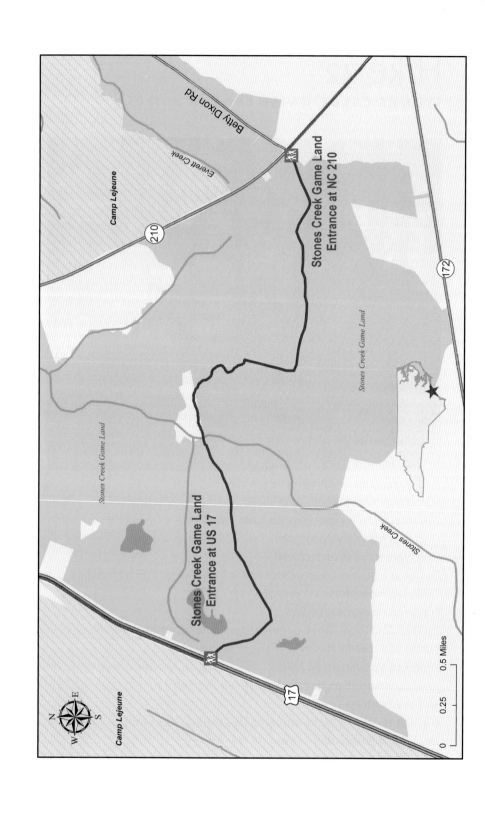

Stones Creek Game Land
Entrance at NC 210

Stones Creek Game Land

Stones Creek Game Land

Stones Creek Game Land
Entrance at US 17

Camp Lejeune

Camp Lejeune

Betty Dixon Rd

Everett Creek

Stones Creek

210

172

17

0   0.25   0.5 Miles

HIKE OVERVIEW

Stones Creek Game Land is a little-known enclave nestled into Camp Lejeune Marine Corps Base. Over the years much of what is now the game land was converted to pine plantation, some of which has been heavily timbered. Under the management of the North Carolina Wildlife Resources Commission, efforts are underway to restore the native longleaf pine savannas that historically grew here. Much of the land through which this hike passes has been planted in young longleaf pine, and gradually hikers will be able to watch it transform into a mature, highly diverse habitat. Even now, the area hosts a diverse abundance of wildlife and plants, including several endangered species.

The hike begins at the back of the parking lot on NC 210, following the main gravel road through the game land. A gate on this road is closed except during hunting season. At mile 1.4, the route turns left from the road onto a smaller track through the woods.

After 2.0 miles, the trail crosses the game land's namesake, Stones Creek, on a long footbridge built by Friends volunteers. It continues on a crude jeep track through an area planted in young longleaf pine, then joins a more substantial road.

At mile 3.1, the road reaches a T-intersection at a lake, which began as a borrow pit for highway construction. This hike and the MST turn right, but hikers seeking a longer walk can turn left on a track that forms a 1.3-mile loop around the perimeter of the lake, always keeping close to its shore. It returns to the main route at the next turn (mile 3.2 of this hike).

Leaving the lake, the hike continues through a mixture of young longleaf pine and remnant pine plantation for approximately 0.3 mile before reaching US 17, the end of the hike.

DRIVING DIRECTIONS

From Jacksonville, go south on US 17. Approximately 11.1 miles beyond the US 17 / NC 24 interchange in Jacksonville is an intersection with NC 210.

To reach Trailhead 1, turn left at this intersection and continue 3.2 miles on NC 210. The trailhead is on the right, across from the entrance to Dixon Elementary School.

To reach Trailhead 2, continue straight on US 17 for 1.9 miles. At the fifth crossover opening after the NC 210 intersection, turn left onto the gated track, where limited parking is available.

HIKE DIRECTIONS

0.0 From the parking lot at Stones Creek Rd. and NC 210, walk on the seasonally gated gravel road to begin this hike.

0.3 Continue straight past a grassy path on the left.

0.5 Continue straight past a prominent fire break on the right.

1.2 Continue on the road through a 90-degree right-hand curve.

1.4 At a post, turn left into the woods.

1.7 Just before reaching a road, turn left into the woods.

1.8 Pass a bench on the right and turn left on a road.

2.0 Cross Stones Creek on a long footbridge, then cross a bulldozed fire break. Continue on a crude jeep track.

2.7 Bear slightly left where the track joins a more substantial road.

2.7 Pass a gate and continue through an open white-sand area, keeping left to remain on the jeep track.

3.1 At a T-intersection at a lake, turn right. *Note*: To the left is a gated jeep track that circumnavigates the perimeter of the lake always keeping close to its shore. This optional scenic loop is 1.3 miles. It returns to the shorter route at the next turn.

3.2 Continue straight on unmarked Deer Ln. at the intersection with the circuit loop road around the lake.

3.4 Continue straight past a dirt track on the right. *Note*: There may be a post at this intersection marking a potential future route for the MST.

3.5 Reach US 17 and the end of this hike.

SPECIAL CONSIDERATIONS

Hunting is permitted in the Stones Creek Game Land during hunting season, generally September through April, Monday through Saturday. If the gates at the game land entrances are open, it is hunting season. We encourage hikers to wear blaze orange whenever hiking during hunting season, but it is not necessary to inform the Wildlife Resources Commission of your presence. Learn about hunting seasons and regulations at www .ncwildlife.org/Hunting before going into the game land.

FOR MORE INFORMATION

Stones Creek Game Land Map: www.ncwildlife.org/Portals/0/Hunting
/Game-Land-Maps/Coastal/Stones-Creek.pdf

Stones Creek Game Land Management Plan: www.ncwildlife.org
/Portals/0/Hunting/GameLand-Plans/Stones-Creek-GLMP.pdf

Hike 33
LEJEUNE MEMORIAL GREENWAY
Montford Point Road to Holcomb Boulevard

Vietnam Veterans Memorial, Lejeune Memorial Gardens.
Photo by Cpl. Jackeline Perez Rivera, United States Marine Corps.

Distance: As desired, up to 9.6 miles round-trip
Degree of difficulty: Easy to moderate
Trail type: Paved greenway
Trailhead: Montford Point Rd., Jacksonville; no facilities
Trailhead coordinates: N34.74739, W77.41511
Trailhead elevation: 16 feet
Total elevation change: gain, 100 feet; loss, 89 feet
MST segment: 15
Highlights: Military memorial garden; rails-to-trails greenway; water views
Dogs: Allowed on leash

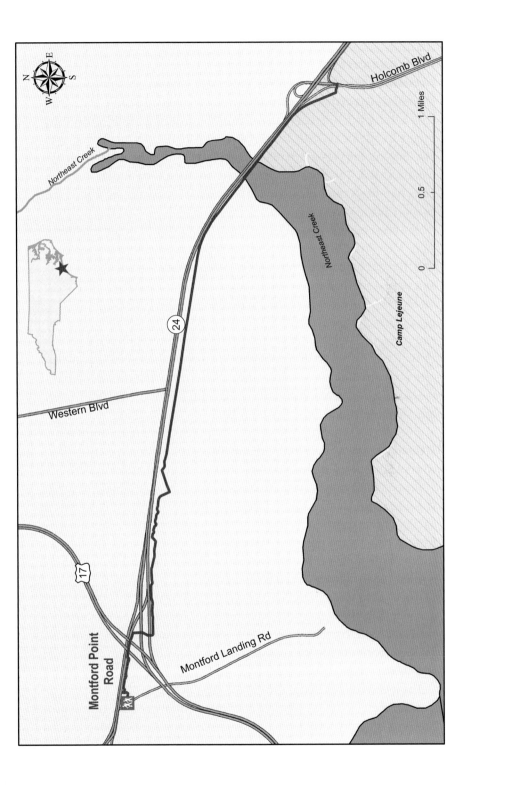

HIKE OVERVIEW

Jacksonville, the site of this hike, is home to one of the nation's largest concentrations of military personnel, at Camp Lejeune Marine Corps Base. The route, which runs along the edge of the base, is a fitting and moving tribute to our nation's servicemen and women. There is no parking available beyond the western trailhead, so the hike must be done as an out-and-back walk. This book provides directions for 4.8 miles of hiking (one-way), but hikers can turn around at any point to make the walk as long or as short as they like.

The hike begins just east of downtown Jacksonville at the edge of the Lejeune Memorial Gardens, on a concrete path that wanders past the memorials. The master plan for the gardens includes the Museum of the Marine and several additional memorials, but the gardens currently hold the Beirut Memorial, in memory of the 273 Marines who lost their lives in an October 23, 1983, terrorist attack on the barracks in Beirut, Lebanon; the Vietnam Veterans Memorial, the second-largest in the country behind only the national memorial in Washington, DC, honoring the nearly 10 million veterans of all branches who served active duty during the Vietnam era; the Montford Point Marine Memorial, dedicated to the first African American Marines, who entered the corps between 1942 and 1949 and served at an adjacent, segregated base, now named Camp Johnson; and the 9/11 Memorial Beam, a beam from the Twin Towers placed in memory of those who lost their lives in the September 11, 2001, terrorist attacks.

Beyond the gardens, the path crosses under multiple bridges of the US 17 / NC 24 interchange, then makes a sharp left turn. From this point, it parallels NC 24 on a narrow corridor between the highway and the marine base. At mile 1.7, the trail turns left and goes through an underpass under one of the entrances to the marine base. Access on the path straight ahead is restricted to military ID cardholders only.

After going through the underpass, the trail reaches a T-intersection, where it joins the Jacksonville Rails-to-Trails Greenway. The MST and this hike head right; the left turn crosses a beautiful pedestrian bridge over NC 24, then continues to Marine Blvd., home to many of Jacksonville's stores and hotels.

The greenway continues to skirt the edge of the marine base through small pockets of forest, crossing four more entrance roads to the base (some no longer in use), before crossing Northeast Creek at mile 3.9. The bridge over the creek provides outstanding views of this estuary.

The greenway continues past a solar panel installation at mile 4.2 and back into the woods before reaching its end at Holcomb Blvd. just outside Camp Lejeune's main gate. Hikers who have made it this far should turn around and retrace their steps.

DRIVING DIRECTIONS

From US 17 North, take the exit for Montford Point Rd., also marked for the memorials.

From US 17 South, take the exit for NC 24 East, to Camp Lejeune and Morehead City. At the end of the entrance ramp, turn right on Business NC 24 West. After 0.4 mile, at the next traffic light, turn left on Montford Point Rd. (Signs before the intersections point to the memorials.) Parking is on the left.

HIKE DIRECTIONS

0.0 From Montford Point Rd., turn into Lejeune Memorial Gardens and begin walking on the Lejeune Greenway.

0.5 Pass under multiple bridges of the US 17 / NC 24 interchange.

1.7 Turn left through the underpass.

1.8 At the T-intersection, turn right onto the Jacksonville Rails-to-Trails Greenway.

1.9 Continue across an old road.

2.4 Continue across a divided road just outside a base entrance gate.

2.7 Continue across a base entrance road, no longer in service.

3.2 Continue across another divided entrance road.

3.9 Cross a footbridge over Northeast Creek.

4.2 Pass a solar panel installation on the right.

4.8 Reach a restricted parking lot off Holcomb Blvd., just outside the main gate to Camp Lejeune. Turn around and retrace your steps to finish the hike.

SPECIAL CONSIDERATIONS

Access to the active military base at Camp Lejeune is very strictly controlled. Do not attempt to leave the greenway and enter the base without authorization. (Fences make this difficult or impossible for much of the length, but even where it may be possible, it is illegal.)

FOR MORE INFORMATION

Jacksonville Rails-to-Trails Greenway Map: jacksonvillenc.gov
/DocumentCenter/View/199

Camp Lejeune Marine Corps Base: www.lejeune.marines.mil

Lejeune Memorial Gardens: jacksonvillenc.gov/648/Lejeune-Memorial
-Gardens

Hike 34

THE NORTHERN NEUSIOK TRAIL

NC 101 to Billfinger Road

Typical Neusiok Trail boardwalk. Photo by Randy Johnson.

Distance: 3.3 miles one-way; 6.6 miles round-trip
Degree of difficulty: Moderate
Trail type: Natural-surface trail
Trailhead 1: Neusiok Trail parking lot, NC 101; no facilities
Trailhead 1 coordinates: N34.86962, W76.80635
Trailhead 1 elevation: 20 feet
Trailhead 2: Billfinger Rd.; no facilities
Trailhead 2 coordinates: N34.84935, W76.78282
Trailhead 2 elevation: 20 feet
Total elevation change: gain, 14 feet; loss, 14 feet
MST segment: 16
Highlights: Diverse coastal-plain forest and swamps; wildlife
Dogs: Allowed on leash

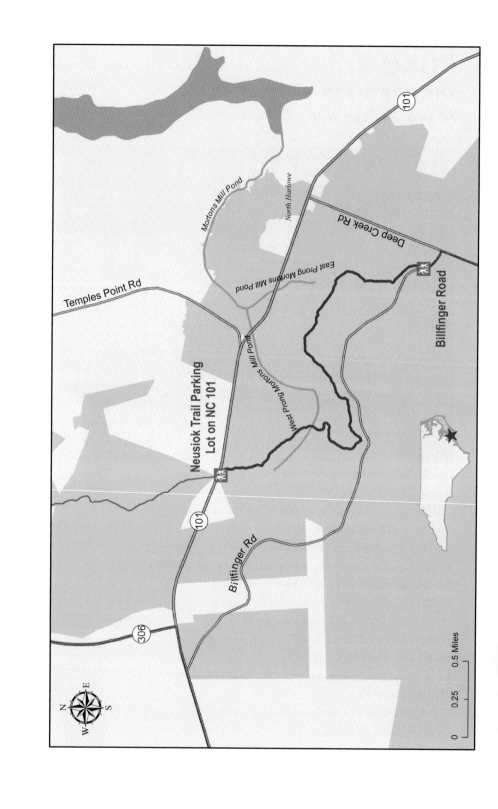

N
W · E
S

Temples Point Rd

Morton's Mill Pond

North Harlowe

Neusiok Trail Parking
Lot on NC 101

East Prong Mortons Mill Pond

Mortons Mill Pond

West Prong

101

306

Billfinger Rd

Billfinger Rd

Deep Creek Rd

Billfinger Road

101

0   0.25   0.5 Miles

HIKE OVERVIEW

The Neusiok Trail, at 21 miles the longest continuous hiking trail in eastern North Carolina, runs concurrently with the MST for its entire length. The Neusiok, which will mark its fiftieth birthday in 2021, was built and is maintained by the Carteret County Wildlife Club with help from the US Forest Service.

The entire Neusiok Trail is within the Croatan National Forest, the only national forest on North Carolina's coastal plain. This hike follows one of the most diverse stretches of the Neusiok. Hikers will encounter several types of pine forest, mostly loblolly, and longleaf pine savanna, as well as hardwood swamps with deep bogs. Boardwalks and bridges take hikers over many of the boggiest areas, but this forest is a wet place. Among the animals making this forest home are black bear, alligator, bald eagles, songbirds like the prothonotary warbler, endangered red-cockaded woodpeckers, and several species of poisonous snakes. The trail also passes the remains of some old tar kilns, now just mounds in the woods, from the days when this area had a thriving naval stores industry.

The hike begins at a small gravel parking area on the south side of NC 101. For the first 0.7 mile, the trail passes through mixed-pine woods before passing the Dogwood Camp Shelter, a camping spot about 250 feet off the trail to the right. For hikers who underestimated their needs, drinking water is available here.

Beyond the shelter, the trail drops slightly into a hardwood swamp—the elevation change is noticeable mainly because of the change of vegetation, not because of any pronounced hill. In the swamp, there are boardwalks over some of the wettest spots and a bridge, built by the Youth Conservation Corps, crossing West Prong Mortons Mill Pond Branch. Returning to pine woods, the trail reaches a junction at mile 1.3, where the MST continues on the left fork while the right fork leads 0.1 mile to Billfinger Rd. The trail briefly drops back down into a swampy area to cross another bridge, this time over East Prong Mortons Mill Pond Branch, at mile 2.8, and returns to pine woods until the end of the hike at Billfinger Rd.

DRIVING DIRECTIONS

From the intersection of US 70 and NC 101 (Fontana Blvd.) in Havelock, head east on NC 101 for 6.4 miles. About a mile beyond the junction with NC 306 is a gravel parking lot on the right, Trailhead 1.

To reach Trailhead 2, continue another 2.0 miles on NC 101, then turn right on Deep Creek Rd. (Forest Road 169) an unmarked sandy road just before the highway makes its second right-hand curve after Trailhead 1. (If you reach the intersection at the little community of North Harlowe, you have gone about 250 yards too far.) Travel 1.0 mile on Deep Creek Rd. to the first road on the right, Billfinger Rd. (Forest Road 147). Trailhead 2 is 300 yards down Billfinger Rd. on the right; parking is along the side of the wide, lightly traveled road.

HIKE DIRECTIONS

0.0 From the back of the parking lot, head into the woods on the signed trail next to a trail kiosk.

0.7 Pass the Dogwood Camp Shelter 250 feet off the trail to right.

0.8 Cross a bridge over West Prong Mortons Mill Pond Branch.

1.3 At a trail junction, turn left, following MST trail markers.

2.8 Cross a bridge over East Prong Mortons Mill Pond Branch.

3.3 Reach Billfinger Rd. (Forest Road 147) and the end of the hike.

SPECIAL CONSIDERATIONS

Heat, humidity, and insects can make this hike unpleasant in the summer. It is recommended for the cooler months, October through May.

Hunting is allowed throughout the Croatan National Forest. See www .ncwildlife.org/hunting for information about seasons and licenses.

Although boardwalks and bridges cross many of the wettest parts of the trail, the Croatan is still a very wet place. Waterproof boots or water shoes are recommended during wet seasons.

FOR MORE INFORMATION

US Forest Service, Croatan National Forest: www.fs.usda.gov/recarea /nfsnc/null/recarea/?recid=48466&actid=63

Map of Croatan National Forest: www.fs.usda.gov/Internet/FSE _DOCUMENTS/stelprdb5403940.pdf

Carteret County Wildlife Club (trail maintainers in this section): www .carteretwildlifeclub.org

Neusiok Trail Site: www.neusioktrail.org

Hike 35
THE SOUTHERN NEUSIOK TRAIL *Oyster Point Loop*

The Newport River from Oyster Point. Photo by Charles Harris.

Distance: 2.8-mile loop
Degree of difficulty: Easy
Trail type: Natural-surface trail, gravel road, and paved road
Trailhead: Oyster Point Campground; water, restrooms
Trailhead coordinates: N34.76078, W76.76168
Trailhead elevation: 7 feet
Total elevation change: gain, 81 feet; loss, 81 feet
MST segments: 16 and 17
Highlights: Estuary views; birds; freshwater swamps; coastal ecosystem
Dogs: Allowed on leash

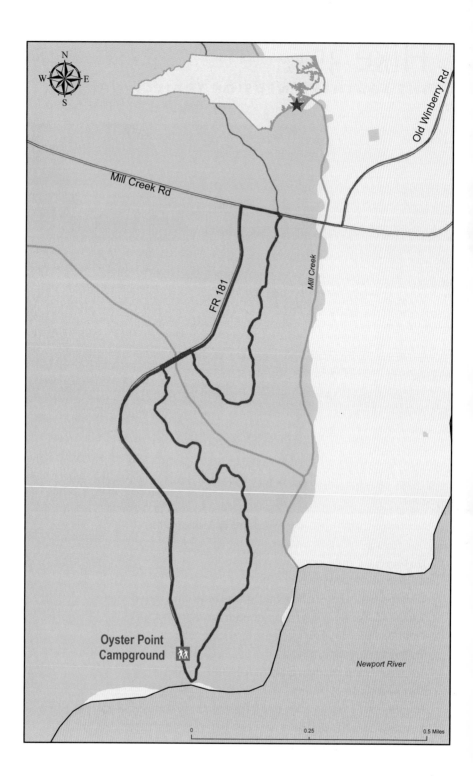

N
W E
S

Old Winberry Rd

Mill Creek Rd

FR 181

Mill Creek

Oyster Point
Campground

Newport River

0   0.25   0.5 Miles

HIKE OVERVIEW

This loop hike includes the southern end of the Neusiok Trail, the longest continuous hiking trail in eastern North Carolina. Along with coastal pine forest and freshwater swamps, the hike offers expansive views of salt marsh and tidal creeks. As with Hike 34, it is entirely within the Croatan National Forest. It begins and ends at the US Forest Service's Oyster Point Campground, the southern terminus of the Neusiok Trail. This book describes the hike as a clockwise route, allowing the hiker to get the road walking out of the way at the beginning and end with the best views.

The hike begins on FR 181, which was also the driving route to the trailhead. Although open to traffic, the dirt road is lightly traveled and makes for pleasant walking through pine forests. After a brief stretch on paved Mill Creek Rd., the hike returns to the woods on a proper trail. Several spots along the way provide vantages over tidal Mill Creek and its associated salt marsh before the trail briefly returns to the forest road to cross a tributary of Mill Creek.

After returning to single-track trail, the hike continues another 0.9 mile through pine woods and along the edge of the marsh. Just before the end of the loop, the trail turns sharply right. A boating access area here provides expansive views over the mouth of the Newport River and creates a memorable end to the walk. From here it is only a few yards back to the parking area and the end of the hike.

DRIVING DIRECTIONS

To reach the trailhead from Beaufort, head north on NC 101 for 10.5 miles, then turn left on Old Winberry Rd. at the sign for Oyster Point. Continue 3.7 miles and turn right on Mill Creek Rd. After 0.2 mile, turn left on FR 181 just past the Carteret County Solid Waste Recycling Site. Continue 1.1 miles to the end of the road and the trailhead.

HIKE DIRECTIONS

0.0 Begin the hike by heading north on FR 181.

1.1 Turn right on Mill Creek Rd.

1.2 After passing the Carteret County Solid Waste Recycling Site but before reaching a bridge over a tidal creek, turn right onto the trail leading into the woods.

1.8 Turn left on a gravel road.

1.9 Turn left on a trail headed into the woods.

2.8 Reach the Oyster Point Campground and the end of this loop hike.

SPECIAL CONSIDERATIONS

Heat, humidity, and insects can make this hike unpleasant in the summer. It is recommended for the cooler months, October through May.

Hunting is allowed throughout the Croatan National Forest. See www .ncwildlife.org/hunting for information about seasons and licenses.

Although boardwalks and bridges cross many of the wettest parts of the trail, the Croatan is still a very wet place. Waterproof boots or water shoes are recommended during wet seasons.

FOR MORE INFORMATION

US Forest Service, Croatan National Forest: www.fs.usda.gov/recarea /nfsnc/null/recarea/?recid=48466&actid=63

Map of Croatan National Forest: www.fs.usda.gov/Internet/FSE _DOCUMENTS/stelprdb5403940.pdf

Carteret County Wildlife Club: www.carteretwildlifeclub.org

Neusiok Trail Site: www.neusioktrail.org

Hike 36

"DOWN EAST" NORTH CAROLINA

Williston to Davis

Trawler and nets near Williston.
Photo by Carolyn Mejia.

Distance: 3.9 miles one-way; 7.8 miles round-trip
Degree of difficulty: Easy
Trail type: Paved road
Trailhead 1: Williston United Methodist Church; no facilities
Trailhead 1 coordinates: N34.78527, W76.50931
Trailhead 1 elevation: 3 feet
Trailhead 2: Davis; several stores with general supplies
Trailhead 2 coordinates: N34.79775, W76.45977
Trailhead 2 elevation: 3 feet
Total elevation change: gain, 6 feet; loss, 6 feet
MST segment: 17
Highlights: Tidal creek crossings; marsh views; rural communities;
    historic store
Dogs: Allowed on leash

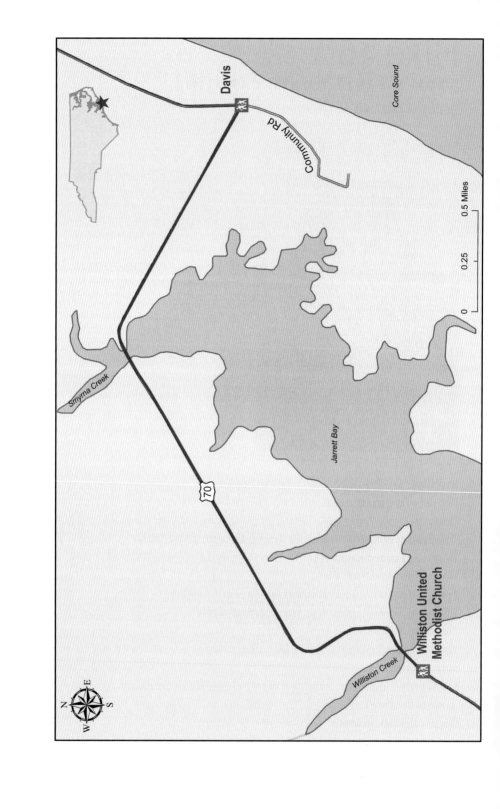

HIKE OVERVIEW

This hike highlights two of the small towns and the coastal ecosystems that exemplify the area that residents traditionally call "Down East." Fishing, particularly for shrimp and blue crabs, is a mainstay of the economy here, and it is not uncommon to see crab pots or shrimp nets along the side of the road.

Beginning from Williston United Methodist Church, the hike is on US 70 eastbound for its entire length. Although a US highway, this road is fairly lightly traveled, and it has wide grassy shoulders. After crossing over Williston Creek, the route enters Williston itself. This tiny village is almost entirely residential.

Leaving Williston, the road continues through salt marsh for the next 2 miles or so. Although much of the marsh has been drained, it still retains some of its native vegetation and can be a good place to see wildlife. A bridge over Smyrna Creek at mile 2.5 provides a little elevation and offers particularly good views of the estuary ecosystem.

After leaving the marsh, the road continues 0.6 mile to the center of Davis, the end of this hike. Davis Shore Provisions General Store, in its historic building on the right, has a coffee bar and sells baked goods, gifts, and clothing and other works by local artists.

DRIVING DIRECTIONS

From Beaufort, take US 70 East, following signs for the Cedar Island Ferry, approximately 14 miles. Trailhead 1, Williston United Methodist Church, is on the left about 0.2 mile past the intersection with Old Nassau Rd. Trailhead 2 is 3.9 miles farther along the same road.

HIKE DIRECTIONS

0.0 Turn left out of the Williston United Methodist Church parking lot onto US 70 to begin the hike.

0.1 Cross a bridge over Williston Creek.

2.5 Cross a bridge over Smyrna Creek, then make an almost 90-degree right turn.

3.7 Pass the Davis Volunteer Fire Department on the left.

3.9 Reach the end of the hike at an intersection in Davis where US 70 turns left.

SPECIAL CONSIDERATIONS

This hike passes through long expanses of wide-open marsh that can be very windy. A windbreaker is recommended gear even on the warmest days.

FOR MORE INFORMATION

Davis Shore Provisions General Store: www.facebook.com/davisshore
   provisions

"Down East" Tourism: www.crystalcoastnc.org/region/down-east

Hike 37

CEDAR ISLAND NATIONAL WILDLIFE REFUGE

Cedar Island High Bridge to Cedar Island
Volunteer Fire Department

Cedar Island National Wildlife Refuge. Photo by Carolyn Mejia.

Distance: 5.9 miles one-way; 11.8 miles round-trip
Degree of difficulty: Easy to moderate
Trail type: Paved road
Trailhead 1: Cedar Island National Wildlife Refuge boat ramp; no facilities
Trailhead 1 coordinates: N34.92575, W76.36470
Trailhead 1 elevation: 7 feet
Trailhead 2: Cedar Island Volunteer Fire Department; no facilities
Trailhead 2 coordinates: N34.97498, W76.29965
Trailhead 2 elevation: 7 feet
Total elevation change: gain, 10 feet; loss, 10 feet (not including the climb over the bridge onto Cedar Island)
MST segment: 17
Highlights: Cedar Island National Wildlife Refuge; marsh and estuary views; wildlife
Dogs: Allowed on leash

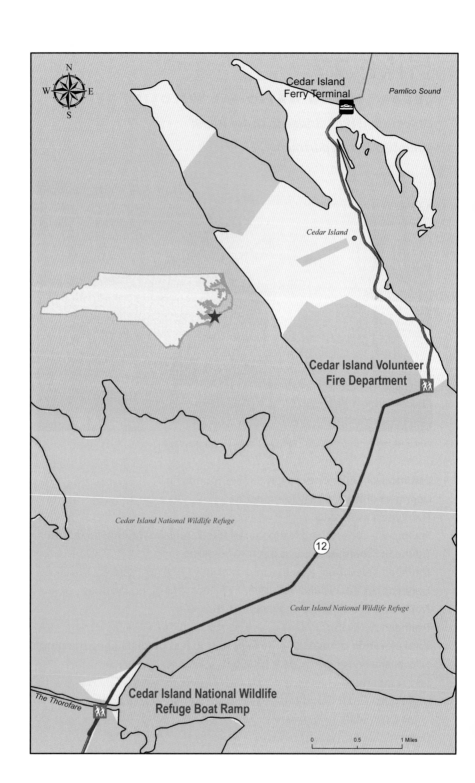

Cedar Island Ferry Terminal

Pamlico Sound

Cedar Island

Cedar Island Volunteer
Fire Department

Cedar Island National Wildlife Refuge

12

Cedar Island National Wildlife Refuge

The Thorofare

Cedar Island National Wildlife
Refuge Boat Ramp

N
W E
S

0   0.5   1 Miles

HIKE OVERVIEW

This hike is almost entirely on a causeway built to carry NC 12 through the salt marshes that make up most of the 14,500 acres of the Cedar Island National Wildlife Refuge. Although the hike is on a roadway, traffic is rarely a problem; almost the only people on the road are visiting the refuge or heading for the ferry from Cedar Island to Ocracoke on the Outer Banks.

The refuge is a remote, almost desolate area: all you can see for miles is grass, water, a few distant trees, and—if the time and conditions are right—vast flocks of birds. The stunning marsh vistas and wildlife-viewing opportunities on this hike more than make up for any isolation. Over 250 species of birds, 91 of amphibians and reptiles, and 35 of mammals are known to live in the refuge, including breeding pairs of black rails, a bird species of special concern. Especially in winter, vast flocks of pelicans, ducks, and other waterfowl are common sights. Secretive birds like clapper rails and marsh wrens are more often heard than seen but are always present.

The hike begins at the parking lot for the Cedar Island National Wildlife Refuge boat ramp. The route returns up the access road and turns left onto NC 12 to cross the bridge over a channel known as the "Thorofare," which separates Cedar Island from the mainland. At the top of the bridge, views stretch for miles over West Thorofare Bay on the left and Core Sound on the right.

After descending from the bridge, the route continues along the causeway through the marsh for 4.4 miles before reaching higher ground, which can be recognized by the presence of trees. The hike goes another 0.5 mile through the woods before leaving the wildlife refuge and reaching the end at the Cedar Island Volunteer Fire Department.

DRIVING DIRECTIONS

From Beaufort, take US 70 East and follow signs for the Cedar Island Ferry, approximately 25 miles. At a well-marked intersection where US 70 turns right to go to Sealevel and Atlantic, continue straight onto NC 12, still following signs to the ferry. Continue 2.9 miles. Then, just before the prominent bridge onto Cedar Island, turn left onto the unmarked driveway for the Cedar Island National Wildlife Refuge boat ramp to reach Trailhead 1. Continue another 5.6 miles on NC 12 to reach Trailhead 2, the Cedar Island Volunteer Fire Department, on the right.

HIKE DIRECTIONS

0.0 From the parking lot, return toward the highway on the access road to begin the hike.

0.3 Turn left onto NC 12 and begin crossing the Thorofare Bridge onto Cedar Island.

0.9 Reach the end of the Thorofare Bridge.

5.3 Continue straight as the road leaves the marsh and continues onto forested land.

5.8 Pass Lola Rd. on the right.

5.9 Reach the Cedar Island Volunteer Fire Department and the end of the hike.

SPECIAL CONSIDERATIONS

The vast reaches of open marshland mean that this can be a very windy place. A windbreaker is recommended gear even on the warmest days.

The bridge to Cedar Island has wide shoulders but no designated pedestrian path. Use caution when crossing the bridge.

FOR MORE INFORMATION

Cedar Island National Wildlife Refuge: www.fws.gov/refuge/Cedar _Island/about.html

Cedar Island National Wildlife Refuge Map: www.fws.gov/uploaded Images/Region_4/NWRS/Zone_3/Mattamuskeet_Complex/Cedar _Island/Sections/About/new%20Cedar%20Island%20Map.jpg

North Carolina Birding Trail: ncbirdingtrail.org/sites/2012/8/1/cedar -island-national-wildlife-refuge.html

Hike 38
CAPE HATTERAS
Hatteras Lighthouse to Frisco Campground

Open Ponds Trail, Buxton Woods.
Photo by Beerdra.

Distance: 5.7 miles one-way (5.6 miles on MST plus 0.1-mile spur);
11.4 miles round-trip

Degree of difficulty: Moderate to strenuous

Trail type: Natural-surface trail and paved road

Trailhead 1: Cape Hatteras National Seashore parking–Park Rd.; no
facilities

Trailhead 1 coordinates: N35.23483, W75.60982

Trailhead 1 elevation: 10 feet

Trailhead 2: Hatteras Island Visitor Center; water, restrooms

Trailhead 2 coordinates: N35.25136, W75.52760

Trailhead 2 elevation: 7 feet

Total elevation change: gain, 154 feet; loss, 151 feet

MST segment: 18

Highlights: Maritime forest; experience of wilderness; tallest brick
lighthouse in US

Dogs: Allowed on leashes no longer than 6 feet

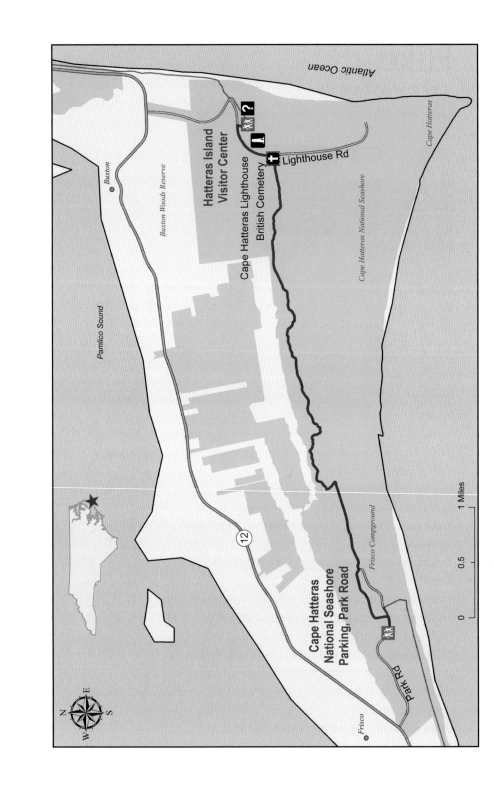

HIKE OVERVIEW

This hike traverses the only significant patch of maritime forest on the MST. The Buxton Woods area comprises 3,000 acres of maritime forest at the southern tip of Hatteras Island that has been spared from development. About 1,000 acres is the Buxton Woods Coastal Reserve, owned and managed by the state of North Carolina. Another 1,000 acres is owned by Dare County or private parties, and the remaining 1,000 acres, which includes the area through which this hike passes, is part of the Cape Hatteras National Seashore. The gnarled live oaks, loblolly pines, dwarf palmettos, and shrubby dunes of the Buxton Woods area create an environment completely unlike the beaches seen by most visitors to the Outer Banks.

In contrast to the pristine forest of Buxton Woods, the eastern end of the hike is at Cape Hatteras Lighthouse, at 210 feet the tallest brick lighthouse in North America, and the most-recognized symbol of the Outer Banks. In 1999, beach erosion forced a relocation of the lighthouse. Over twenty-three days, the lighthouse was slowly moved 2,900 feet west from its original site. The relocation path is still visible and is the continuation of the MST route eastward from this hike. In the new site, the lighthouse is open for climbing in the summer.

The hike begins at the Hatteras Island Visitor Center, adjacent to the lighthouse. The visitor center has restrooms, water, and a small museum and bookshop; it is open 9:00 A.M.–5:00 P.M. every day except Christmas. The route remains on paved roads for 0.6 mile before reaching the Open Ponds Trail at a small parking area.

Just beyond the parking area, the trail passes the British Cemetery, a gravesite for British sailors killed in World War II. This seemingly anomalous cemetery exists because during both World War I and World War II, German U-boats often lurked off the Outer Banks, waiting for attack orders that never came and also forming a blockade. Allied forces, including the British Navy, engaged with the submarines, and several ships were sunk in nearby waters; the casualties were sometimes buried on Hatteras and Ocracoke Islands.

For the next 4.3 miles, the trail follows the Open Ponds Trail through maritime forest, passing a pond at mile 2.1. At mile 5.0, the trail emerges to the Frisco Campground, where the route turns right to follow the loop road through the campground. After passing through the campground entrance, the road reaches a parking area on the left and the end of the hike.

DRIVING DIRECTIONS

To reach Trailhead 1 from NC 12 in Buxton, turn south on Lighthouse Rd., which is prominently marked for the Cape Hatteras Lighthouse. Drive 1.1 miles, then turn left into the driveway for the lighthouse and visitor center.

To reach Trailhead 2 from NC 12 near Frisco, turn south (left if driving from Buxton to Frisco) on Park Rd., which is almost directly across from the Frisco Native American Museum and has signs for the airstrip and campground. Continue 1.0 mile to the parking area on the right. There is also a small parking area near mile 5.6 of the hike, inside the campground. If Park Service personnel will allow you to park there, this can save walking some of the less interesting portions of the trail; however, because they often do not allow this, we have described this hike using the more reliable parking area.

HIKE DIRECTIONS

0.0 From the Hatteras Island Visitor Center, head out the access road toward Lighthouse Rd.

0.1 At a T-intersection, turn left on Lighthouse Rd.

0.2 Pass a parking area for a picnic area and the trailhead for Buxton Woods Trail, a 0.75-mile self-guided nature trail, on the right.

0.3 Continue straight past Loggerhead Ln. on the right.

0.6 At a small parking area with signs for the MST and World War II British Sailor Cemetery, turn right onto the Open Ponds Trail, then pass the cemetery on the right.

0.8 Continue straight past a trail on the right.

1.0 Continue straight past a trail on the right.

1.2 At a Y-intersection, bear left to stay on the main trail.

1.6 Pass Open Ponds Trail MP 1.

2.1 Pass a pond viewpoint on the right.

2.6 Pass Open Ponds Trail MP 2.

3.6 Pass Open Ponds Trail MP 3.

4.0 Continue straight on the sandy track past a sign where a trail comes in from the right.

4.1 Continue straight where a horse-trail sign points left. (The correct trail is marked by an MST sign.) Emerge into a clearing in front of a maintenance building and water tank and turn right on the grassy track.

4.6 Pass Open Ponds Trail MP 4.

5.0 Just after emerging onto a paved road, turn right at a T-intersection onto the Frisco Campground loop. Continue through the campground, staying left at every opportunity until mile 5.6.

5.6 Turn right at a small roundabout, then continue straight through the Frisco Campground entrance gate. *Note*: There is a small parking area about 100 yards to the left of the roundabout. If campground personnel allow it, it may be possible to park here instead of at the trailhead.

5.7 Pass a beach access road on the right, then reach the parking lot on the left and the end of the hike.

SPECIAL CONSIDERATIONS

Mosquitos and other biting insects can make hiking unpleasant any time of year. Insect repellent is recommended.

Much of the trail is on loose sand, which can make walking difficult.

The parking area on Park Rd. can fill up early on summer days, so plan accordingly.

Although hunting is allowed in neighboring Buxton Woods Coastal Reserve, it is prohibited in this portion of the National Seashore.

FOR MORE INFORMATION

Outer Banks Chamber of Commerce: www.outerbankschamber.com

Outer Banks Tourism: www.outerbanks.org

OuterBanks.com tourism site: www.outerbanks.com

NC Department of Transportation NC 12 Facebook page: www.facebook .com/NCDOTNC12

Cape Hatteras National Seashore Maps: www.nps.gov/caha/planyour visit/maps.htm

Buxton Woods Coastal Reserve: portal.ncdenr.org/web/crp/buxton -woods#visitingbw

Cape Hatteras Lighthouse climbs: www.nps.gov/caha/planyourvisit /lighthouseclimbs.htm

Hike 39

OUTER BANKS WILDLIFE AND BEACHES

Pea Island National Wildlife Refuge Headquarters
to Marc Basnight Bridge

Beach walking at Cape Hatteras
National Seashore.
Photo by Pamela Ireland.

Distance: 5.4 miles one-way; 10.8 miles round-trip
Degree of difficulty: Easy to moderate
Trail type: Beach and natural-surface trail
Trailhead 1: Pea Island National Wildlife Refuge Visitor Center parking lot;
  supplies, restrooms
Trailhead 1 coordinates: N35.71603, W75.49329
Trailhead 1 elevation: 7 feet
Trailhead 2: Cape Hatteras National Seashore parking lot just south of
  Oregon Inlet; no facilities
Trailhead 2 coordinates: N35.76701, W75.52574
Trailhead 2 elevation: 7 feet
Total elevation change: gain, 111 feet; loss, 111 feet
MST segment: 18
Highlights: Wildlife at Pea Island National Wildlife Refuge; beach
  walking; historic Oregon Inlet Life-Saving Station
Dogs: Prohibited in Pea Island National Wildlife Refuge west of NC 12;
  otherwise allowed on leashes no longer than 10 feet

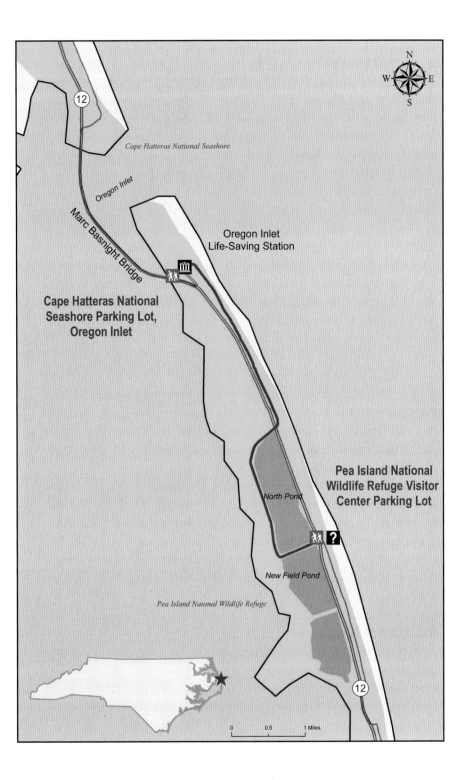

Cape Hatteras National Seashore

Oregon Inlet

Marc Basnight Bridge

Oregon Inlet
Life-Saving Station

Cape Hatteras National
Seashore Parking Lot,
Oregon Inlet

Pea Island National
Wildlife Refuge Visitor
Center Parking Lot

North Pond

New Field Pond

Pea Island National Wildlife Refuge

0   0.5   1 Miles

N
W   E
S

HIKE OVERVIEW

With the only true beach walking in this book, this hike combines two of the best-known aspects of the Outer Banks: the ocean and wildlife. The hike begins at the Pea Island National Wildlife Refuge Visitor Center, which has restrooms, exhibits, and a shop. Stop inside to find out about recent wildlife sightings. It is generally open 9:00 A.M.–4:00 P.M. daily, but it is staffed by volunteers, so hours are subject to availability.

Not part of this hike, but off the beach directly across from the visitor center, a shipwreck is visible at low tide: the *Oriental*, a steamship used as a federal transport ship during the Civil War, sank just offshore in May 1862.

The hike begins from the south end of the parking lot, passing the restrooms on a wooden boardwalk. The first 2.5 miles of the hike skirt the edge of the wildlife refuge's North Pond, a 390-acre artificial impoundment that hosts thousands of migratory waterfowl and shorebirds at certain times of the year. In all, more than 365 species of birds have been recorded at Pea Island.

At mile 2.5, the route crosses NC 12 and heads out to the beach, still within the wildlife refuge. (There is another small parking area here for hikers who want to shorten the walk.) On the beach, shorebirds, gulls, and terns abound, and endangered sea turtles nest during the summer. (Do not disturb any nests or feed or harass any animals; it is not only obnoxious and potentially dangerous but also illegal.)

After 2.6 miles along the beach, the hike passes the historic Oregon Inlet Life-Saving Station. Built in 1898, this striking building is the third on the site, which was one of the original Outer Banks stations. The building is not open to the public, but visitors can walk around it. From the life-saving station, it is a short walk across the dunes to the parking lot near the foot of the Marc Basnight Bridge, and the end of the hike.

DRIVING DIRECTIONS

From Nags Head, drive south on NC 12 and cross the Marc Basnight Bridge over Oregon Inlet. The entrance to Trailhead 2 is on the left immediately after the bridge. Continue another 3.9 miles and turn right into the entrance for Pea Island National Wildlife Refuge to reach Trailhead 1.

HIKE DIRECTIONS

0.0 From the Pea Island National Wildlife Refuge Visitor Center parking lot, begin the hike on the wooden boardwalk just left of the restrooms at the end of the lot.

0.1 Turn right onto a concrete path.

0.6 At the wildlife observation tower, descend from a berm and turn right onto a service road. Follow the service road around the pond.

2.5 Cross NC 12 and then cross dunes.

2.6 Turn left on the beach.

5.1 As you see the historic Oregon Inlet Life-Saving Station to your left, head inland before the inlet.

5.2 Pass the historic Oregon Inlet Life-Saving Station on the left.

5.3 Just before a path leads to a pond, turn left on the smaller path through the dunes.

5.4 Reach the parking lot and the end of the hike.

SPECIAL CONSIDERATIONS

Tides are a major consideration here. A reasonably wide beach at low tide may be completely covered at high tide. Tide tables should be considered an essential tool for this hike (the last item in "For More Information" is an online tide table for the area).

FOR MORE INFORMATION

Outer Banks Chamber of Commerce: www.outerbankschamber.com

Outer Banks Tourism: www.outerbanks.org

OuterBanks.com tourism site: www.outerbanks.com

NC Department of Transportation NC 12 Facebook page: www.facebook.com/NCDOTNC12

Pea Island National Wildlife Refuge: www.fws.gov/refuge/pea_island

Pea Island National Wildlife Refuge Map: www.fws.gov/southeast/pubs/Pea_tearsheet.pdf

Outer Banks Bird List: www.fws.gov/southeast/pdf/bird-list/pea-island-national-wildlife-refuge.pdf

North Carolina Birding Trail: ncbirdingtrail.org/sites/2012/8/1/pea-island-national-wildlife-refuge.html

Oregon Inlet Life-Saving Station: uslife-savingservice.org/station

/endangered-stations/oregon-inlet-life-saving-station-1898
-rodanthe-nc

Oregon Inlet Bridge Tide Table: tidesandcurrents.noaa.gov/tide
_predictions.html (search for "Oregon Inlet Bridge")

Hike 40
JOCKEY'S RIDGE STATE PARK

Matt Loomis finishing the MST at Jockey's Ridge. Photo by Johnny Massey.

Distance: 0.5 mile one-way; 1.0 mile round-trip
Degree of difficulty: Easy
Trail type: Sandy trail
Trailhead: Jockey's Ridge State Park; water, restrooms
Trailhead coordinates: N35.96369, W75.63263
Trailhead elevation: 10 feet
Total elevation change: gain, 82 feet; loss, 13 feet
MST segment: 18
Highlights: Highest and largest dunes on East Coast; eastern terminus
 of MST; views of the ocean and sound
Dogs: Allowed on leashes no longer than 6 feet

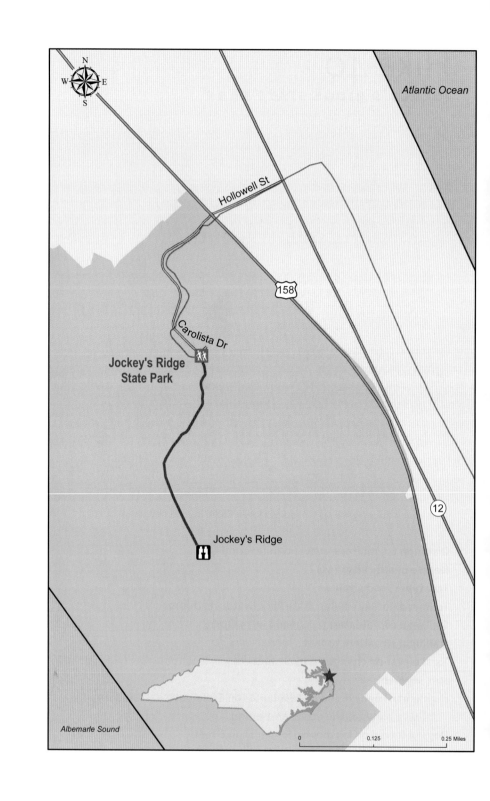

Atlantic Ocean

Hollowell St

US 158

Carolista Dr

Jockey's Ridge State Park

Jockey's Ridge

NC 12

Albemarle Sound

| 0 | 0.125 | 0.25 Miles |

HIKE OVERVIEW

Like Hike 1 (The Great Smokies: Clingmans Dome to Fork Ridge Trail), this hike has special significance to Friends of the MST, because it includes the eastern terminus of the trail. The hike is special in its own right, however. Although short, it provides an experience quite different from anything else on the MST as it ascends the tallest and largest active dune complex in the eastern United States, up to 60 feet tall.

The top of the dunes commands views far over the Atlantic Ocean and Albemarle Sound, as well as up and down the Outer Banks. Not far from here is Kill Devil Hills, where Wilbur and Orville Wright made their first powered flights. Unsurprisingly, hikers at Jockey's Ridge often encounter hang gliders launching from the dunes. Kite flying and sand-boarding are also popular activities at the park.

The hike begins from the right side of the Jockey's Ridge State Park Visitor Center, which is open every day from 9:00 A.M. to 6:00 P.M. (but to 5:00 P.M. November–February, and closed Christmas Day). The visitor center has water, restrooms, and a museum.

Following MST blazes, the trail begins in maritime forest, but it quickly emerges to the dunes. From here, the MST crosses bare sand dunes, which constantly change with the winds. There is no definitive route; the goal—the eastern terminus of the MST—is simply wherever the highest point on the dunes is.

DRIVING DIRECTIONS

From US 158 (also known as S. Croatan Hwy.) approximately 4.5 miles north of its intersection with US 64, turn west onto Carolista Dr. (called Hollowell St. on the other side), which serves as the park driveway. Continue about 0.2 mile to the parking area.

HIKE DIRECTIONS

0.0 From the right side of the visitor center, follow the trail marked for the MST into the woods.

0.5 Reach the highest point of Jockey's Ridge State Park, which is also the eastern end of the MST, then return to the visitor center.

SPECIAL CONSIDERATIONS

Shoes are highly recommended, as the dunes harbor sandspurs and sand temperatures may be as much as 30 degrees hotter than air temperatures.

FOR MORE INFORMATION

Outer Banks Chamber of Commerce: www.outerbankschamber.com

Outer Banks Tourism: www.outerbanks.org

OuterBanks.com tourism site: www.outerbanks.com

NC Department of Transportation NC 12 Facebook page: www.facebook .com/NCDOTNC12

NC State Parks Jockey's Ridge State Park: www.ncparks.gov/jockeys -ridge-state-park

Jockey's Ridge State Park Map: files.nc.gov/ncparks/maps-and -brochures/jockeys-ridge-state-park-map.pdf

Friends of Jockey's Ridge State Park: www.jockeysridgestatepark.com

EPILOGUE THE FUTURE OF THE MST

Like all long-distance trails, the "current route" of the Mountains-to-Sea Trail changes steadily as new trail opens and we are able to more and more closely approximate the "planned route," a vision developed by North Carolina State Parks and its partners for a continuous, off-road MST. In the last twelve years alone, more than 200 miles of that planned route have opened, and new sections of trail are added each year.

As new trail opens, Friends of the MST tries to immediately shift the connecting "current route" to incorporate the new trail sections. Sometimes, however, large gaps between trail sections or dangerous roads prevent us from immediately adding new trail into the route that long-distance hikers follow now.

In the meantime, these trails that will be incorporated into the MST in the future are also great places to explore. Here's a sampling:

URBAN MST LOOP IN THE WINSTON-SALEM AREA

The planned route of the MST includes an alternate loop that will run through the towns of Tobaccoville, Bethania, Winston-Salem, and Kernersville. Although this loop does not yet connect, several miles of the future route exist already and can be enjoyed now.

Bethania. The town of Bethania—established by Moravians in 1759—has over 4 miles of natural-surface trail in four sections ranging from 0.7 to 1.4 miles in length. These natural surface trails offer great opportunities for short hikes, with a focus on history.

Winston-Salem. The Salem Creek Greenway and Salem Lake Trail are part of Winston-Salem's municipal greenway system, which boasts 25 miles of paved and unpaved trails spread across the city. The Salem Creek Greenway is a paved path running along the city's south and east sides for 5.2 miles. At its east end, it connects to the Salem Lake Trail, a 7-mile, mostly unpaved path that encircles Salem Lake.

THE HAW RIVER TRAIL FROM GRAHAM TO SAXAPAHAW

The planned route of the MST is to follow the Haw River from the Haw River State Park in Rockingham County to Saxapahaw in Alamance County. Already 8 miles of this route has been incorporated into the current route from the Indian Valley Golf Course in Burlington to the Town of Haw River. Several other sections of trail along the planned route are worth exploring now. One of these is a 1.75-mile trail in Saxapahaw, a former mill town in rural Alamance County that has reemerged as a center of art, culture, music, food, and outdoor activities. Another is the 5-mile trail system in Shallow Ford Natural Area. Other trails in the area offer opportunities to create loops and extend hikes.

NEUSE RIVER LAND ROUTE

One of the most exciting parts of the planned MST route is the vision of creating a continuous land trail paralleling the Neuse River from the Falls Lake dam to the Neusiok Trail near Havelock. The Neusiok and 35 miles of trail from Raleigh to Clayton and in Smithfield have already been incorporated into the current route. While work continues to build trail in other areas, Friends of the MST recognizes paddling the Neuse from Smithfield to the Neusiok as a way to complete that portion of the MST. Several sections of walking trail have now opened in this area.

Goldsboro. The 3.3 miles of designated MST route in Goldsboro include Center St. through downtown, a connection along Ash St., and the unpaved Stoney Creek Greenway.

Cliffs of the Neuse State Park. Over 4 miles of trail run through this beautiful park, which features unusual coastal-plain geology. Multicolored cliffs towering 90 feet above the Neuse River contrast with pine and oak forests and cypress swamps, and wildlife abounds.

Kinston. This burgeoning food, art, and outdoor recreation destination features the Riverwalk, a half-mile-long greenway along the banks of the Neuse that connects several facilities including a band shell, the farmers market, and the CSS *Neuse II*, a replica of a Confederate gunboat built and sunk during the Civil War.

New Bern. The former colonial capital of North Carolina has over 3 miles of trail, passing by several of the city's historic locations, in several sections along the shores of the Neuse and Trent Rivers.

NORTH RIVER WETLANDS PRESERVE

In Carteret County as the MST heads toward the Cedar Island ferry to the Outer Banks, the current route passes the entrance to the North Carolina Coastal Federation's North River Wetlands Preserve and its 8 miles of trail. This preserve is one of the largest wetland restoration projects in North

Carolina, and the trail there is to be incorporated into the current MST route as soon as connecting trails can be built.

These represent just a few of the many exciting additions planned for the MST. For more information, including maps and planning documents, please visit the "Future Plans" of Friends' website, MountainstoSeaTrail .org/the-trail/future-plans.

ACKNOWLEDGMENTS

Many friends of the Mountains-to-Sea Trail have helped to make this book possible. In 2012, the Board of Directors of Friends of the MST decided to start the process of writing a trail guide for the entire trail. That guide was written first as individual chapters for each of the trail's nineteen segments. Beginning in 2014, they were published, first in electronic format only, and then in three regional books. Early contributors included Carolyn Sakowski, a Friends board member and chair of the Documentation Committee that led the initial efforts; Danny Bernstein, Crawford Crenshaw, Kate Dixon, Mark Edelstein, Jim Grode, Bob Hillyer, JoEllen Mason, George Poehlman, and Robert Trawick, who scouted trail segments and wrote chapters; John Lanman, a Friends board member and MST completer who edited drafts; and PJ Wetzel, the first person to scout what became the Coastal Crescent route of the MST. It is no exaggeration to say that without their efforts and the resulting guides, this book could not exist.

We also owe a debt of gratitude to all the photographers who provided images for the book, either by entering our photo contests or by sending photos specifically for this guide. They are too many to list, but they have made this book immeasurably more beautiful.

Our cartographer, Curtis Belyea, took on a monumental task while also undergoing and recovering from knee surgery. His hike maps provide a clarity that text alone cannot, and we appreciate his dedication to the cause.

Finally, we thank our editorial team at UNC Press—Mark Simpson-Vos, Jessica Newman, Kim Bryant, Mary Carley Caviness, and Cate Hodorowicz. Special thanks to Christi Stanforth, who turned half-formed ideas into coherent book sections, cleaned up our sloppy prose, and fixed mistakes. (Of course, Friends remains solely responsible for any remaining errors.)

APPENDIX 1   MST SEGMENTS

Segment 1: Peak to Peak—Clingmans Dome to Waterrock Knob

Segment 2: The Balsams—Waterrock Knob to Pisgah Inn

Segment 3: The High Peaks and Asheville—Pisgah Inn to Black Mountain Campground

Segment 4: Gorges, Peaks, and Waterfalls—Black Mountain Campground to Beacon Heights

Segment 5: The High Country—Beacon Heights to Devils Garden Overlook

Segment 6: The Elkin Valley—Devils Garden Overlook to Pilot Mountain State Park

Segment 7: The Sauratown Mountains—Pilot Mountain State Park to Hanging Rock State Park

Segment 8: Rivers, Railroads, and Lakes—Hanging Rock State Park to Greensboro's Bryan Park

Segment 9: Revolution and Textiles—Greensboro's Bryan Park to Eno River State Park at Pleasant Green Road

Segment 10: Eno River and Falls Lake—Eno River State Park at Pleasant Green Road to Falls Lake Dam Near Raleigh

Segment 11: Neuse River Greenways and the Let'Lones—Falls Lake Dam to Howell Woods Environmental Learning Center

Segments 11A–16A: The Neuse River Paddle Route—Smithfield to the Neusiok Trail

Segment 12: Agricultural Heartland—Howell Woods Environmental Learning Center to Suggs Mill Pond Game Land

Segment 13: Carolina Bay Country—Suggs Mill Pond Game Land to Singletary Lake State Park

Segment 14: Land of History—Singletary Lake State Park to Holly Shelter Game Land

Segment 15: The Onslow Bight and Jacksonville—Holly Shelter Game Land to Stella

Segment 16: The Croatan and Neusiok Trail—Stella to Oyster Point Campground

Segment 17: Down East North Carolina—Oyster Point Campground to Cedar Island Ferry

Segment 18: The Outer Banks—Cedar Island Ferry to Jockey's Ridge State Park

APPENDIX 2 COMPLETING THE MST

Friends hopes that completing the hikes in this book will inspire some readers to take on more of the MST, perhaps even completing the entire route from Clingmans Dome to Jockey's Ridge. Hiking the entire MST can provide a great sense of accomplishment, but the other rewards it offers may be even greater. As Ian "Wolfpack" Fraher, a 2010 completer, said, "I fell in love with North Carolina! The natural wonder, rich history and southern hospitality all contributed to the experience."

There are two approaches to completing the MST: thru-hiking or section hiking. A thru-hiker starts at one end and hikes, with no significant inter-ruptions, to the other end, while a section hiker hikes sections of the trail in no particular order or time frame, often intermittently, eventually complet-ing the entire trail. Each approach has its advantages and disadvantages.

At our annual meeting each year, Friends of the MST awards a certifi-cate to everyone who completes the trail. We recognize a few different methods for completing the trail. Because stretches of the MST are still on back roads and bike routes, completers have the option of hiking or biking the road and paved greenway sections (although we encourage walking greenways). They also have the option of paddling the Neuse River (Seg-ments 11A–16A) to complete the Coastal Plain section from Smithfield to the Croatan National Forest near Havelock. To qualify for the completion award, however, a hiker must walk all natural-surface trail sections of the MST unless the paddle option is chosen.

The Friends website has many additional resources for completers, in-cluding information about timing, planning, preparation, budgeting, and "trail angels" who can make the challenging logistics of hiking the MST a little easier. Information specific to completers is mostly on the FAQ page (MountainstoSeaTrail.org/the-trail/faqs) and "Hiker Resources" (Mountains toSeaTrail.org/the-trail/hiker-resources). In addition, we encourage hikers to contact us before beginning their journeys. We like to know who is on the trail, and we can provide additional resources and information, includ-ing making connections with others who have done it before.

The MST completer community is tight-knit. Another thru-hiker, Me-lissa "Queen of the MST" Thompson, noted, "The central form of currency among people along the trail was kindness and respect." We invite you to join our community.

INDEX

ABOUT FRIENDS OF THE
MOUNTAINS-TO-SEA TRAIL

Friends of the Mountains-to-Sea Trail, based in Raleigh, North Carolina, is the primary nonprofit organization supporting and advocating for North Carolina's flagship hiking trail, the 1,175-mile-long Mountains-to-Sea Trail. Friends' mission is to bring together communities and volunteers to build a simple footpath connecting North Carolina's natural treasures for the enjoyment and education of people.

Friends supports the trail in four primary ways: (1) building and maintaining trail through volunteer-based task forces; (2) enhancing the trail route by identifying and implementing people and facilities to make the hiking experience more pleasurable; (3) encouraging people to use the trail by spreading the word to interested groups and providing information resources such as this guide; and (4) expanding support by helping elected officials—local, state, and federal—and citizens understand the value of the trail for recreation, quality of life, the economy, and the environment and providing information about how to make the trail happen. Learn more about Friends and the MST, or get involved, by emailing info@MountainstoSeaTrail.org or going online at MountainstoSeaTrail.org.

Jim Grode, who is Friends' trail resource manager, grew up in the Piedmont of North Carolina and currently lives in Asheville with his wife. An environmental lawyer by training, he is an avid hiker and trail runner who explores the MST on a weekly basis.

Other **Southern Gateways Guides** you might enjoy

Southern Snow

The New Guide to Winter Sports from Maryland to the Southern Appalachians

RANDY JOHNSON

The ultimate guide to winter sports in the South

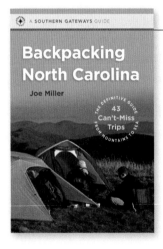

Backpacking North Carolina

The Definitive Guide to 43 Can't-Miss Trips from Mountains to Sea

JOE MILLER

From classic mountain trails to little-known gems of the Piedmont and coastal regions

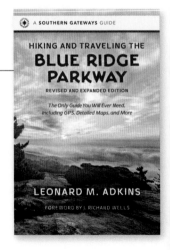

Hiking and Traveling the Blue Ridge Parkway, Revised and Expanded Edition

The Only Guide You Will Ever Need, Including GPS, Detailed Maps, and More

LEONARD M. ADKINS

Revised and Expanded Edition
Foreword by J. Richard Wells
All you need to know about the Blue Ridge Parkway

Available at bookstores, by phone at **1-800-848-6224**, or on the web at **www.uncpress.org**